INDIAN DAYS
OF THE LONG AGO

The camp of the Salish

INDIAN LIFE AND INDIAN LORE

INDIAN DAYS
OF THE
LONG AGO

By Edward S. Curtis
Author of "The North American Indian"

ILLUSTRATED WITH PHOTOGRAPHS BY THE
AUTHOR AND DRAWINGS BY F. N. WILSON

YONKERS-ON-HUDSON, NEW YORK
WORLD BOOK COMPANY
1915

TAMARACK PRESS

ISBN 0-913668-45-1

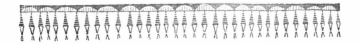

FOREWORD

THIS little book was written in the hope that it would give a more intimate view of Indian life in the old days, in the days when to the far western tribes the white race was but a rumor, and buffalo roamed the plains in countless numbers. A further desire was to call attention to the great divergencies in Indian life, the number of languages, and the striking differences in dress and habits. The pictures, as well as the text, will emphasize this.

We have been prone to regard Indians as being without religion or spiritual life. Instead of being without a religion, they were influenced in every important act of their life by spiritual beliefs and religious practices. This fact is touched upon not as a pedantic lecture but rather as we see its influence on the characters of the story and in the folk-tales. I have tried to show how their religious beliefs influence the character building of the youth. Simple animistic beliefs, which bring the spirit beings close, are easy of comprehension, and the belief in the ever-present nearness has a strong influence upon the children. What could be more powerful in character building than the mountain vigil of Kukúsim? This story of fasting and prayer is not a created play of words, but is given practically as told by those who have thus fasted.

The character He Who Was Dead And Lives Again has its historical prototype in a wanderer, a dreamer, a cataleptic who was able at will to throw himself into a state of trance; a leader in spreading the cult of hypnotic religious practices of which the great Siouan Ghost Dance of 1889 was an example.

The Huron, introduced to give a glimpse of the life of the eastern Indians, is fully as logical, since in the Flathead country—the central scene of the story—there are many direct descendants of the old eastern wanderers who came to this region at the date of the story. In fact, it was the old wanderers from the east who gave the thought of the oncoming hordes of white people.

In brief, the story is told quickly from a full heart, drawn from a store of thoughts and lore, gathered through half a lifetime of intimate contact with many tribes in many lands. It has been a labor of love, and I can only hope that my readers will from the reading derive a small part of the happiness that I have derived from its writing.   *The Author.*

CONTENTS

x   *Contents*

INDIAN DAYS OF THE LONG AGO

INDIAN DAYS OF THE LONG AGO

PROLOGUE

THE camp of Lone Pine, chief of the Salish, or Flatheads, was on the banks of the Red Willow River, a beautiful stream flowing through the forests of the Bitterroot Mountains, in what we now call western Montana. Its cold, translucent waters come from the springs and snows far up among the mountain crags.

Beautiful lodges or tepees made from the dressed skins of buffalo and elk were scattered everywhere among the pines.

The village was like the camps of hundreds of other Indian chiefs or head men, which stood beside the forest stream, by the quiet brook of the open plain, by the lake in the mountains, or on the grassy bank of the prairie lake.

A camp site was never adopted by chance, but was chosen for a definite purpose. In some cases the object was fishing; in others to hunt the buffalo, or elk and deer; or to dig roots and gather berries and other wild fruits.

MORNING IN CAMP

THE hour is that of a new day, just before the sun lifts itself from the forested peaks to the  eastward. Here and there low voices of mothers speak to children; a woman calls to another to be awake, and not to hold too long upon the sleep. Now the smoke curls upward from the lodge-tops, and from fires built in the open just outside. To the nostrils comes the fragrant odor of burning pine. Soon the savory smell of roasting meat will tell that the women are preparing the morning meal.

There is a hushed feeling of excitement and anticipation. Only yesterday rumor came to the chief of two strange wanderers who on this day would reach the camp. In color they were said to be like the Salish, but their words were different. They told of strange people, of strange lands; they sang unknown and curious songs. They talked

with the spirit people, and claimed much knowledge of the spirit world. But most wonderful of all, they said they could see into the future, and they made prophecy of disaster to all the tribes. Long into the night just past had Lone Pine and his head men sat about the council fire and discussed the strange rumor.

With the waking of the camp, Lone Pine, dressed in his trappings of a chief at ceremonial times, came from his lodge. He mounted his horse, and rode slowly about the camp, acting as his own herald.

In a loud voice he cried: "Hear ye! Hear ye! Chiefs! Men! Women! Boys! Awaken! Do not hold on to your sleep like lazy ones, but listen to my voice! This is a great day for us! The two strange men with wonderful stories will reach our camp before the sun sinks. It is said that one of these men was born by the Big Water from where the West Wind comes. Not alone does he tell us of the land of the West Wind, where the Sun sleeps, but he has traveled to the land of the South Wind, which brings summer.

Lone Pine

He has seen curious people, in color like ourselves, but living in strange ways.

"The other wanderer comes from the Big Water of the East Wind, where the Sun rises. He has wandered for many winters, and has seen strange people and their ways. Of all these people they will tell us.

"Chiefs, my words are heavy with meaning to our nation. The stories these wanderers tell are of many brown people like ourselves. But, besides, they tell of a people with skins of snow: a people as countless as the sands, who will take our land, steal our daughters, and try to teach us new ways. It is a story of war, misery, and sickness to our nation!

"Women, make clean the camp and our lodges! Prepare much food, that our guests and our men may have a great feast! Young men and warriors, dress as is fitting for greeting the visitors to our camp! Your chief has spoken! I have said it!"

Kukúsim, the son of Lone Pine, had sat in the

shadows at the council fire on the previous night
and had listened wide-eyed to the words of his
father and the head men.
He was early awake, at-
tending to the words of
the chief as he rode about
the camp on his proud
war-horse. Many of his
father's words were of
matters too deep for his
understanding, but he
realized that this was a
great event in the life of
his people, and he wished
that he, like his e l d e r
brother, were man grown,
that he might be counted
a m o n g the w a r r i o r s,
a m o n g the men who
could protect the people
however great the dan-
ger. He often dreamed

Kukúsim

of performing some great feat in battle and having his name changed from Kukúsim, the Star, to
something more warlike, such as Kills First, or
Hunts The Enemy.

Soon his mother was saying: "My son, come
with Sister, and eat food. Eat plenty, that
you may grow up strong. Remember your
grandfather's teachings, and do not make a
loud noise. If you do, no one will take you

Blue Bird

for children of a chief."

The mother was of the Pierced Nose tribe,[1] who lived far to the southwest. She was very proud of her children. One, a boy of fifteen winters, was already a man allowed to go on hunting and war expeditions with his father. Kukúsim, who was less than ten, still clung to his mother and the interests of her life. The sister, Blue Bird, had come into the world two winters later, and was still his companion. Baby was a boy, and had been with them but two summers, and young as Blue Bird was, she called herself "little mother" to the baby.

At breakfast time Baby was still asleep, so Blue Bird was carefree. Kukúsim and she sat close together in the family circle about the food, which was in two or three horn and wooden dishes placed upon the ground. The mother saw

---

[1] This tribe is known to us as the Nez Percés, which is French for "Pierced Noses." Many of the men in this tribe wore a slender shell, shaped like a dog's tooth, in a hole cut through the partition between the nostrils. Therefore other tribes called them the Pierced Noses.

that they had plenty of the best of the food. Besides, she made a point of giving them some of the roast elk ribs, on which there was little meat, admonishing them: "Gnaw the meat from these bones, children. It will make your teeth strong and white."

While Kukúsim was picking the meat from his rib bone, his favorite dog crept up and coaxed for it. The boy watched his mother, and when she was looking in another direction, he gave his bone to the dog. Just at that moment his mother looked around, and seeing himself detected, Kukúsim exclaimed, "Mother, my dog was very hungry!"

Like a true Indian mother, she laughed as she scolded him, and as punishment she gave him no more meat for his breakfast. But Blue Bird, sorry for Brother, shared her food with him.

As soon as the two children had finished their morning meal, Kukúsim said: "Mother, I shall find my friends Scarface, Yellow Hawk, and Rabbit, and we will take our bows and arrows

An Indian sweat lodge

to the forest to hunt birds, squirrels, and rabbits."

Before he left the lodge, Sister whispered to him: "I shall get my friends and we will make a play camp just at the edge of the woods. When you are coming home, stop there and show us what you have killed, and we will play at cooking it for our husbands."

Before breakfast Kukúsim had gone with his father to bathe in the river. This was a daily practice, not only to keep their bodies clean, but to harden them so that they could endure cold and changing weather without discomfort or illness. It was summer time, but owing to the snows in the mountains and the cold nights, the water was icy cold. This, however, did not discourage the Indian chief, who with his son plunged in and swam about for a time. They stepped out on the bank, and as the day was warm, sat in the sun and dried themselves. Had it been a winter day, they would have wrapped a blanket or robe

about them. Many Indian tribes bathed in this
way every day, summer and winter. In some
places they had to cut holes in the thick ice, but
still the daily bath was not omitted. In that
way the boys grew up with sturdy bodies, able
to withstand all sorts of hardship.

Soon the boys were away to the forest. Each carried a small bow, and in a skin quiver were  his arrows. Some of these had points of sharpened stone or bone; some had wooden points; others were blunt ended, for bringing down game without killing it so that the boy could capture it alive. The boys wore no clothing but a loin-cloth of skin, with or without the hair upon it. This not only hardened and strengthened their bodies, but left them free to chase their prey.

The chief's son, Kukúsim, was looked up to as the leader, so he called out, "Let us go to the rabbit traps, and see what we have caught."

Scarface and Yellow Hawk agreed at once: "That is what we will do. There will be something in at least one snare."

But Rabbit declined to go, saying that he did not care to see the snares.

"We know," chaffed Yellow Hawk, "why Rabbit does not want to go with us to the snares. He is named after the rabbit, and he is afraid we have caught one."

Kukúsim, always careful of the feelings of his companions, quickly arranged the matter by

suggesting that Rabbit and Scarface go toward
the grove of the partridges, while he and Yellow Hawk visited the snares.

With Yellow Hawk close behind him, Ku-
kúsim f o l l o w e d the trail
along the river. Then turn-
ing off, he walked through
the forest to the higher and
more open ground, where
the rabbits lived, and where
the boys had their snares.

Said Yellow Hawk: "Ku-
kúsim, I do not think we
shall have any rabbits today. I think Rabbit has
given us bad luck by wishing that we might not get
any in our traps. After this we will not take
him with us when we want rabbits."

The first snare they found sprung, but
empty. They reset it carefully and went on
their way. The second one was broken and
pushed aside.

"What has done this, Yellow Hawk?" whis-
pered Kukúsim. "Let us look closely and see.
The ferns and grass are broken in this direction.
We will follow."

They came to a wet, soft piece of ground,
where they saw great tracks in the soft
earth.

"It was a bear," exclaimed Kukúsim. "His

The river near the camp

tracks are broader than my two hands, and beside them are the tracks of a baby bear."

"Let us go back out of this thicket," exclaimed Yellow Hawk. "Perhaps the mother bear and her cub are still close."

Kukúsim felt the cold creeping up and down his back, but being a chief's son, he knew that he must be brave and show courage whether he had it or not. So, though his knees were shaking and his voice was hushed, he insisted that they go on to the next trap.

"Let us walk quietly," he cautioned. "Then if the bear is about, she will not hear."

Suddenly Kukúsim stopped in the trail. "Look, Yellow Hawk, what is that?" he whispered.

There, beside the trail in front of them, the two boys saw a bear digging skunk-cabbage. Her head was so far down in the hole she had made that she had not heard them. Then the cub caught sight of them and crowded close up to the mother bear, who knew by this that there

was danger. She lifted her head, and with a snort jumped into the brush.

For a moment Kukúsim and Yellow Hawk stood close together without speaking. Then Kukúsim proudly boasted: "I was not afraid! See how the bear ran! Let us go on now, to our next snare, and if there is nothing in that we shall know that the wishes of Rabbit have been heard."

This was their fourth snare. They had been taught by the old men that in setting traps they should have four, as this was the sacred number of the four winds and the four cardinal points. The fourth trap also was sprung and empty. Convinced now that good fortune was not with them in snaring rabbits, they counseled what was to be done.

"If this happened to our fathers," urged Kukúsim, "they would sing songs to drive away the evil and to bring good fortune."

"We know many songs, but we do not know

a song for bringing us good fortune in snaring rabbits," protested Yellow Hawk.

"I have heard my father say that the best songs are those which are made in the forest," answered Kukúsim. "Let us make a song to the rabbits."

Still fearful of the bears, Yellow Hawk suggested that they also make a song to the mother bear. So they made up a song to the bear, and another to the rabbits, and sang them four times. This is what they sang to the bear:

> "Shaggy One, who walks like a man!
> Long Claws, who digs like a woman!
> Be happy, be not angry with us!"

And this is the way the music is written down:

And thus they sang to the rabbits:

"White Tails, swift are your feet.
Come to our traps, for we wish your bodies.
Fine feathers then will we give to your spirits."

And this is the way the music is written down:

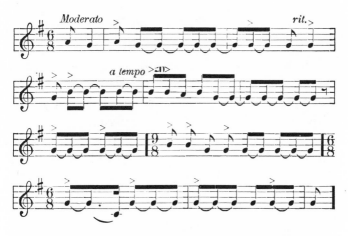

"Now let us find the other boys," said Kukú-sim. "But the songs belong to us, and we will not tell about them."

After traveling through the woods for a time, they came to a small opening in the pines. In the center of this was a large rock, and here they stopped to find some sign from their companions. Sure enough, there on the flat surface of the stone were a few broken twigs, two brown pebbles, and a freshly peeled piece of bark with two or three black marks upon it.

To a white boy this would have meant nothing. Even with the Indian boy there was much question as to just what the message was, but with some study they made out that two partridges had been killed with arrows, two deer tracks seen, a badger chased into his hole, and that the other boys had gone to the lake for duck nests.

A DISPUTE

IN a short time Kukúsim and Yellow Hawk, who had no difficulty in finding them, were with their companions on the rush-grown shore of the lake. Several nests had already been found, but it was not the purpose to take the eggs, because in two moons these eggs would be plump young ducks, easy of capture. Tiring of the search for duck nests, they decided to go to a small creek that emptied into the river. Here there were always trout to be taken.

In the tiny stream, so narrow that in many places they could jump across it, they looked for the deep, dark pools. There they lay down on their stomachs on a sharp bank or overhanging log, and extended their arms fully into the water. Soon the trout swam close by. The boys slipped their hands gently under the fish,

and suddenly closed their fingers about the gills.

Before long each boy had enough fish for an ample meal for his family, and they decided to go down to the river for a swim.

The morning bath with father and the other men was merely a ceremony; for a lark it must be a warm afternoon, and just boys. The water was icy cold, but they were accustomed to that. They dived, and they played all sorts of games. They were like fish in the water, for their parents had taken them to the stream when they were mere babies, and as they learned to walk and talk they also learned to swim. After their frolic they sat on the bank in the sun to warm, and then swam again.

Something besides the lowering sun reminded the boys that the day was passing. In the excitement of play, food at midday might be easily overlooked, but when the day was done they were always ready for the evening meal.

The four comrades had not, however, gone entirely without food since breakfast, as during the day they had found many varieties of bulbous roots, tender plant stalks, and luscious berries.

As they started for the camp, they remembered the excitement there, and the expected visit of the two strange men.

"Let us hurry, that we may reach camp before these men arrive," urged Kukúsim, "and to-night while they are in council we will creep back in the dark shadows where we shall not be seen, and listen. Let us hear what these men are to tell."

Now it must be remembered that almost every Indian tribe had a language of its own, different from the speech of its neighbors, and either largely or totally unintelligible to them. So the Indians of the prairies and the mountains invented a system of signs, by which they could converse rapidly and accurately, just as deaf mutes talk with their hands. The sign language is still used when Indians of different tribes meet.

"Will they talk with our own words?" asked Scarface.

"No," replied Kukúsim, "my father says they will talk only with their hands."

Rabbit complained, "I do not understand much of the hand-talk."

"That is your own fault, Rabbit," answered

Kukúsim. "You are lazy and will not try. Your father says in council: 'My son sleeps while I try to teach him to dance. His feet do not play in the air, but drag like stones on the ground.' Rabbit, you will never make a great warrior like your father unless you wake up!"

Rabbit's face burned with anger and humiliation. "Kukúsim, you think you are smart because your father is a chief, and the men say you can hand-talk like old men, and dance so that all the people want to watch you. When it comes to the day of the war party, that dancing and hand-talk will not get the honors that make chiefs."

"Rabbit, your feet will be as heavy in war as they are in dancing, unless you listen to your father and be awake. And now that I have said my hard words, I will make you happy by promising to tell you tomorrow all that is said tonight, and to help you in learning to talk with your hands."

At the edge of the woods they passed the play lodge of Blue Bird and her companions. It was just like the real lodges, only much smaller, and here the girls spent hours playing as little mothers.

Catching sight of the boys, Blue Bird called: "Bring us your game! We will cook it, and pretend that you are men and hunters, bringing home to their wives the game and fish that they have caught."

"We will give you a few of the smaller fish, Sister, but all the rest we will take to our mothers and grandmothers, to show them that we are really becoming men, and can hunt the game and catch the fish as well as our fathers and grandfathers did."

So with some banter and boy-like teasing, they went on to the camp. As they passed each lodge, they caught sounds of an unusual nature. Words were low and earnest, and they could see warriors passing from lodge to lodge, carrying garments and ornaments worn only on great occasions, such as a dance or a feast. When they caught glimpses of the interior of a lodge, they saw men dressing in ceremonial costumes of white deerskin and gay feathers, and men and women painting their faces.

The camp was alive with expectation. The boy hunters quickly caught the spirit, and almost forgot that they were bringing their mothers the game of a day in the forest.

At the lodge of the chiefs Kukúsim's mother greeted them with a smile, and encouragingly said, "Really, our sons are becoming men!"

Then she warned them not to make loud noises, so as to disturb the chief and his head men, who were in council.

"The strangers are coming, and there is much need of serious talk," she said.

GREETING THE STRANGERS

Kukúsim slipped up to the door of the lodge and looked in. His father, in his medicine [1] costume, was sitting in his accustomed place of honor at the back of the lodge, and on both sides of him were other chiefs, each dressed in his best garments. Their words were low and quiet. Lone Pine filled the pipe, lighted it,

[1] The word "medicine" here means supernatural, or anything supposedly of a supernatural nature. A medicine-man is one who is believed to cure illness by magic, through the power given him by some supernatural being with whom he has talked in a vision. A medicine shirt is one worn by such a healer when performing his cures. Medicine songs he uses while calling upon the spirits for help, and a medicine dance is a ceremony for the purpose of driving sickness away from the whole tribe.

MEDICINE SONG OF THE EAGLE

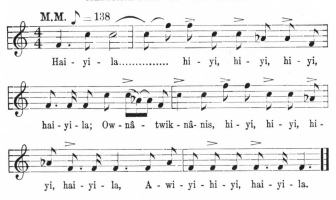

M.M. ♪ = 138

Hai - yi - la............... hi - yi, hi - yi, hi - yi,

hai - yi - la; Ow - nâ - twik - nâ- nis, hi - yi, hi - yi, hi -

yi, hai - yi - la, A - wi - yi - hi - yi, hai - yi - la.

Tilting on wings, flapping, flapping, flapping, tilting on wings:
Pursuing by means of song, flapping, flapping, flapping, tilting on wings,
Soaring high, tilting on wings.

23

Fasting in winter

and then passed it about the circle for all to smoke.

A warrior stood up and said: "It is not for me to speak of this with big words. If I did, my brothers might say, 'Yellow Cloud has small thoughts behind large words.' Black Eagle, when he fasted on the high peaks of the mountains, was shown great visions by the spirit people. Let him talk. The visions told him much. His courage in battle brought him many honors. Let Black Eagle speak. I have finished."

Black Eagle, slowly and with deliberation, stood upon his feet. His height was the breadth of a hand more than that of the others. On his head was a close-fitting, crestlike cap made from an eagle skin, and wrapped close about him was a robe of the buffalo. As he rose, the robe was thrown off, and he stood before his fellows like a bronze statue.

"Brother chiefs of the Salish, Yellow Cloud has spoken of my long fasting in the summer and in the bitter winter. Many visions have been granted me, but this is not the time to speak of them. Today two strangers come to us. They have many stories to unfold. When we have heard the words which come from afar, we will give deep thought and then speak. It is time we were ready to meet and make welcome the visitors. I have said it."

Lone Pine rose to his feet, and the words of his strong voice were

Black Eagle in his robe

these: "Black Eagle has spoken well. It is time we should mount our horses and prepare to welcome our visitors. Around the council fire tonight we will talk. Running Owl, ride about the camp and tell our young men to be ready."

Running Owl quickly mounted his horse, and as he rode he called out repeatedly: "Our chief bids you be ready! Soon the scouts will re-

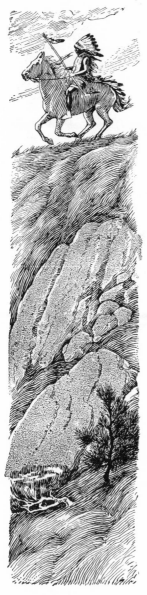

port the coming of the strangers. Mount your horses and be ready!"

Scarcely had the herald started when the chief and his head men mounted their horses and began riding around just inside the camp circle. All were singing Lone Pine's songs. Each moment, as they rode, other men joined the cavalcade, and soon every man in the camp was in the party. And now they rode away to the plain where the visitors were to be met. They passed through open groves of pine, and came upon a flower-dotted meadow, a place which afforded a broad outlook. There they halted and waited for word from the scouts.

Their eyes were scarcely less penetrating than those of an eagle, and soon they saw a mounted scout. He was on a high crest, outlined against the sky, and

he rode back and forth on the same line. This was the signal that he had sighted the newcomers. Now he turned his horse and rode madly toward the warriors.

Lone Pine and his chiefs were all in line, slightly in advance of the main party; at such times ordinary warriors remained behind their chiefs. The scout galloped up, dismounted, and reported to the chief that the two strangers were on a far-away hill; that they had halted some time ago to sing many songs, paint their bodies, and put on their fine clothing.

Lone Pine listened quietly until the scout had told his story. "Chiefs and warriors," he shouted, "what this scout tells us is good. We know he speaks with a straight tongue. It was a true report that told us these men were important men, with great knowledge of spirit things; for has not our scout seen them while they sang their songs and talked with the spirit people? Now we will ride to meet them. To show that we are warriors, we will spare not our horses. We will sing the songs of your chief."

For a time they rode slowly, and then, coming close to where the visitors were, they broke into the wild gallop of warriors. Soon they sighted the travelers, who were mounted on their gaily bedecked horses and sitting like statues outlined against the sky.

As the warriors reached them, each one endeavored to be the first to strike with a coup-stick.[1] This desire to be the first to touch the newcomers brought about a brief whirlwind of struggling horses and shouting men, and had not the visitors known of the friendly intentions of the warriors, they would certainly have thought themselves at the last moment of their lives.

After this first mad rush the warriors drew back, that the chiefs might have conversation with their guests. There was only an exchange of greetings here, as all seri-

[1] In many tribes, especially of the Prairie Indians, each warrior carried into battle a long staff decorated with fluttering eagle-

ous subjects must be put off until they gathered around the council fire.

Now they all started upon the return to camp. Lone Pine and Black Eagle, as the leading chiefs, rode at the head of the column, and beside them the strangers. The lesser chiefs, the scouts, and the other warriors came close behind.

As the returning party reached the camp, they all began to sing, and rode round and round the camp circle, not rapidly, but in a slow and stately

---

feathers and scalps. This was the coup-stick (pronounced *coo*-stick). The first part of the word is the French *coup*, meaning "a blow" or "stroke."

It was a high honor for a warrior to strike an enemy lightly with this staff, because in so doing he ran great risk of being killed while using a harmless stick instead of a bow or a spear. This is what is called "striking a coup." In their dances and speeches the men always boasted of their great deeds, enumerating each one. This is known as "counting coups." Warriors ranked according to the number and the daring of their coups.

In rushing upon visitors and striking them with coup-sticks the Indians were only imitating warfare, just as a sham battle imitates a real fight.

fashion. The women and children, all dressed in their finest clothes of deerskin decorated with colored porcupine quills and elk teeth, stood beside the lodges watching the cavalcade.

In the center of the camp the women had pitched the long lodge. This was made by taking the poles and skin covers of many lodges and combining them into one long structure. The poles and skins of twenty-five lodges had been used, making one about a hundred and fifty feet in length and twenty-four feet in width. This was a council lodge of ten fires. That is, when the council met at night ten fires burned at intervals down the middle of the floor. The usual family domicile had but one fire. There were also lodges of two fires, or of any other number up to ten. While the council lodge stood, the families who had furnished single lodges to make up the large one usually lived in the big structure.

Lone Pine, the proud chief, was master in this council lodge, but he had not taken down his home to help build it. He was rich in skins and lodge coverings, and furnished his share without destroying his home.

When the riders had encircled the encampment several times, the chief and the visitors stopped before the home of Lone Pine, and the other men went their individual ways to join their families. As they rode up to their lodges and dismounted, the women or boys took charge of the horses, as that was a part of their work.

The chief now called an invitation for certain men to come to his lodge, to take food with his guests. These men were ten or twelve in number, and each was invited by name.

On succeeding days it would be the privilege of other important men to ask the visitors to be their guests, and to call out the names of those they wanted to honor by inviting them to the feast with the strangers. At every such feast the host gave presents to his stranger guests, and sometimes to the others as well.

THE COUNCIL LODGE

With the coming of darkness, people from all parts of the camp began to gather at the council lodge. That none might be absent, a crier was sent to shout the command that all were to dress and attend the council.

Kukúsim and Scarface were eager to learn about the strangers, and slipped quietly into a place close against the walls of the lodge, but well up toward the end where the chiefs would sit.

The entrance was at the middle of one side, and all the important men sat in a half-circle at one end. The hundreds of spectators sat on the ground at both sides of the long lodge. Down the central space were the fires which gave light.

When the people were all assembled, Lone Pine, sitting in the center of the curving line of chiefs, filled the pipe.[1] He lighted it, and after

one puff from the long stem passed it to the man at his left. This man passed it on to the left, and so it was handed from man to man until it reached the last one of the chiefs. He placed the stem to his lips and drew a whiff of smoke, which

[1] With the Indians, smoking in council is not for pleasure, but is a serious and solemn ceremony.

he blew toward the ground, saying in a low voice, "Earth, to you I smoke!" Then he blew upward another draft of the smoke, saying, "Sky, to you I smoke!" He blew smoke to each of the spirits of the winds—the East Wind, the South Wind, the West Wind, the North Wind.

This done, he passed the pipe to the man at his right, who also smoked to the Earth, the Sky, and the Four Winds. So it went on from man to man, until it came back to the chief. He smoked as the others had, and refilled and re-lighted the pipe. It was now passed from man to man to the right until it reached the last man on that side. He smoked in the same way, and started the pipe on its return toward the chief, who, upon receiving it, placed it on a buffalo skull in front of him and rose to his feet.

"Two moons ago," began Lone Pine, "a party of our hunters returned with word of two great and wise medicine-men who were with a hunting

A man of the Apsaroke

expedition of the Apsaroke.[1] To this news I gave much thought. I said in my heart: 'Let us see and counsel with these medicine-men. Perhaps they can give us power which will strengthen our tribe and give victory in battle.' So I sent our brave young warrior, Fast Elk, to ask these wise men to visit us. Fellow chiefs, was that well?"

"Aye! Aye! Aye!" voiced all those in council.

"We know that in their hearts are many strange things which they can tell us. One night is not enough to hear it all. We want them to stay with us many moons, perhaps many winters. They will learn that the Salish are brave and fear no enemy, that the hearts of our women are warm, and their words as gentle as the mur-

[1] The Apsaroke (pronounced Ap-sa′-ro-kĕ), as they call themselves, are usually known as the Crow Indians. They are a bold, hardy tribe, living in south central Montana, and formerly also in northern Wyoming.

mur of the brook. Brother chiefs, make our guests welcome! Prepare many feasts for them! Give them the softest of your robes for their bed! They will tell us how to live and be big over our enemies.

"I have taken horses twice from the Apsaroke, twice from the Piegan,[1] once from the Snakes.[2] One Piegan have I killed and scalped. In honor of these my deeds I give to each of our guests five horses. I have said it."

During Lone Pine's speech one of the Salish chiefs rapidly translated to the visitors by means of the sign language, and at the end five short willow rods were handed to each guest as visible tokens of the gift of the horses.

Now stepped forward Black Eagle. "Lone Pine, our chief, has spoken well. Our visitors have seen the lands from which all winds come. In their many fastings in strange places they have learned secrets which make their power great. We want to keep them with us, that we

---

[1] The Piegan were a large, warlike tribe of northern Montana.

[2] The Snakes, or Shoshoni, roamed over what is now Wyoming, southern Idaho, and northern Nevada.

Looking to the land of the winds

may grow to be a greater people, that we may succeed in war, that we may have our wives and children well and strong. We want to hear their voices in council. We want to hear their songs of war and their songs to the spirits. From their counsel our young men will know better how to fast in the high mountains.

"Salish chiefs, warriors, make our guests welcome!

"All the Salish know that twelve winters ago in the buffalo country I rode unarmed among our enemies, the Piegan, and struck their chief with my coup-stick. Of another Piegan I have the scalp! From a camp of the Snakes I captured a horse while it stood tethered at the door of its owner's lodge. These were men's deeds. In honor of them I now give to each of our guests a horse, a lodge, and robes! I have said it!"

Little Bear stood up. Many winters had piled their snows about his lodge, and the winds of many summers had laid deep wrinkles in his face. Every tribesman knew his strength and courage. His tongue was as sharp as the claws of a bear, and fear of his cutting words brought close attention from every man in council. Before beginning to speak he turned toward the guests, and in sign language said:

Little Bear

"I am called Little Bear, because with these two hands I killed the largest bear in our mountains."

Then with fire in his voice he began his rapid speech:

"Salish chiefs, I speak now. I fear lest our words be foolish words. Are we to stand here tonight and each count his coups? Lone Pine and Black Eagle will tell us that we are here

Lean Wolf

to learn of the strangers, but you spend the time talking of your deeds, of ponies, and of gifts. Countless times we have heard these tales, until our youths have for amusement woven them into song. Are we to have our ears made weary with stories older than a toothless bear? Let us hear the words of the strangers! I have said it!"

The chiefs were glad that Little Bear had made his words so brief. Well they knew how he could hold them up to ridicule if he saw fit.

Lean Wolf, a warrior as old and wrinkled as Little Bear, with scars of countless battles, stepped forward.

"Little Bear's tongue is sharp, like the arrow-point, and were he less brave, his words would find no one to accompany them with laughter. And were he as wise as brave, he would soften a nest for his aged bones with smiles and words of honey. It is easy to get laughter with words which cut like the bear's claw, but they do not bring friends. There is, however, I say, much truth in his speech. Let us cease our talk, and ask the strangers to tell us of the things known to them. Do I speak right, brother chiefs?"

"Aye! Aye! Aye!"

Once more the pipe was filled and smoked in the regular way, and was replaced on the buffalo skull.

THE STORY OF THE TWO STRANGERS

ONE of the visitors stood up. In appearance he was unlike the other Indians about him. He was less tall, his face was broad, his shoulders were more massive, and his hips narrower than theirs. For an instant he stood hesitating. Then with his hands he said:

"Salish, I do not do the hand-talk well. Where I was born we did not use this way, but as I have grown old I have learned to make my hands speak.

"I know many words of the Salish, not just as you with your tongues make them, but nearly. My father's people were neighbors of those who, though far away, speak words almost like yours. So as I talk with my hands I will also give such words as I can, and that will help you to understand.

"My name is He Who Was Dead And Lives Again. My winters are so many that I have no count of them, but I know that the strength which made my feet as light as the deer's has gone from me. In my numberless winters and summers I have seen many things, — seen them when I was alive, seen them when my body lay as though dead and my spirit was elsewhere. All these things I will in time try to tell you, but I cannot retravel the trails of a lifetime in one night.

He Who Was Dead

"My parents were of the people who live by the Big Water where the sun goes down, where the forest is thick and dark, where people travel always in canoes, large and small. Many, many tribes are there. My father's tribe is called the Clayoquot.[1] There, a

[1] The principal village of the Clayoquot (pronounced Clah'-yo-quŏt, but usually mispronounced Clä'-ku-ŏt) was on Meares Island, off the west coast of Vancouver Island, British Columbia. The village was called Tla-o'-qui, and the people Tla-o'-qui-ŭt, which the whites turned into Clayoquot. Meares Island is named after an English explorer who visited this coast in 1788 and 1789, and Vancouver Island for a captain of the British navy who sailed around the island in 1792.

young warrior, I was captured by our enemies. Fearful that I should escape, they carried me far away and sold me to others. Again I was sold and taken far across the snow mountains, where flows the Great River [Columbia], and where the lodges are covered with rushes and skins. My heart was sore with longing for my home and people.

"But soon I gazed into the dark eyes of a maiden, and no more did I think of my old home. The son of the chief also looked with love upon the maid of my choice. He demanded my life. This the chief refused to grant, exclaiming: 'You, a chief's son, and cannot win the maid of your choice without my putting a slave to death! No maid would want a man with so weak a heart!'

"The young man was angered by his father's

words, and he counseled with other youths how to make away with me. Without the knowledge of the chief, they crept upon me while I was fishing at night with a dip-net, and hit me from behind. The first blow did not kill me, and we fought for a time. Then a blow made my body dead, but my mind

was alive. I could hear their words, but could not move. They spoke of what to do with my body. The decision was to put me into a canoe and set me adrift on the river. 'Then my father,' reasoned the chief's son, 'will think he has stolen the canoe and fled.'

"In the canoe I drifted on waters slow and fast. I heard the roar of a rapid, and tried to make my spirit move my hand, but of no avail. My body was still dead. Then the canoe lurched and pitched, shot into the air, and half filled with water; and still I drifted on. My eyes were like my body, dead; but I knew that night had changed to day, and that the sun was shining in my face. Still I drifted. Day changed into night, and once more it was day. Then I heard the soft voices of women and felt the jar of a canoe touching mine. I knew but few of the words they spoke. At first they thought me dead.

"Then one said: 'Sister, he is not dead. He is only in the shadow land. What a handsome man!

Sister, we will take him home and have songs made to call back his spirit. Then perhaps one of us will have him for a husband.'

"They towed my canoe ashore, and I felt myself being carried into a house. There was much excitement, and many people talked at once. Then a medicine-man began to sing, and to blow life into my body, and to work my arms and chest. At last strength began to return to me, and I could open my eyes.

"Many were the questions as to whence I came, but it was long before the strength of words came to my tongue. The singing man told me it was well that the maids had found me, as just below was the great waterfall, where the angry waters would have devoured my canoe. Laughing, he said: 'They have saved your life. They can have you for a slave or a husband.'

"And still my heart was heavy with the thought of the maiden far up the river.

"Days passed. Strength came to my limbs, and I thought I had escaped from the clutches of the evil spirits, when again my body became

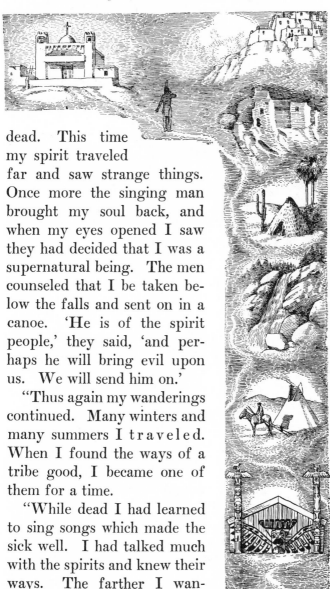

dead. This time my spirit traveled far and saw strange things. Once more the singing man brought my soul back, and when my eyes opened I saw they had decided that I was a supernatural being. The men counseled that I be taken below the falls and sent on in a canoe. 'He is of the spirit people,' they said, 'and perhaps he will bring evil upon us. We will send him on.'

"Thus again my wanderings continued. Many winters and many summers I t r a v e l e d. When I found the ways of a tribe good, I became one of them for a time.

"While dead I had learned to sing songs which made the sick well. I had talked much with the spirits and knew their ways. The farther I wandered the stranger the people, the stranger their ways, the more curious the plants, the grass, the fruit. For many winters my steps were toward the wind of the south. Then I turned my feet toward the new-born sun. I crossed a great river [Colorado], and traveled on.

Indians of the palms

"Strange sights were before me. The houses were not of boards, not of rushes, not of skins, not of leaves. They were of stones, one built high upon the other."

At this strange statement his listeners were wide-eyed. "Truly," thought they, "can such things be not of dreams?"

The old man continued: "There are greater wonders than stone houses. Do you know that the people of the stone houses call the snakes their brothers, and clasp them to their bosoms, and

The Snake Brothers

take them in their teeth, and that no snake ever does harm to a single one of the people?"

A murmured "Ah! Ah! Ah!" swept over his listeners. "Truly, that is medicine!"

Now stronger grew the voice of the speaker. "But, Salish, stranger things than Snake Brothers saw I there,—men like us in form, but like snow in color, of strange ways and words, and strange songs and religion. They are proud. They look down upon our ways and say we must make our songs and religion like theirs. Their talk says the white brothers are like the grains of sand, that when a handful is taken away, others quickly take their places. Long I talked with one of these white men, and my heart became heavy.

"I sang to the spirits. Then my body became dead again, and my spirit saw many things. In my vision I saw these white men, like the countless buffalo, swarm across the land. I saw them

build their houses by the rivers and the springs.
I saw them taking our forests and killing our
game, until the red men, women, and children
cried for food. I heard children wail, I saw warriors and mothers sick with famine and disease.
Then woe, woe! I saw all the nations of our
land cry out, reaching their hands to the spirit
people. And the cry brought no answer!

"When my body awoke again, I talked long
with the white song singer, and told him of my
vision.

" 'You saw right,' was his reply. 'The red man
must give his country to the white. The red
man's songs are not true songs. They lead him
on crooked trails.'

"Then he told me of his songs and prayers,
but I lost the trail and could not follow him. All
I could answer was: 'My songs and my prayers
are good enough for me. Long before you
white skins with your great songs have taken
our lands, I shall have started on the long trail
to ghost land.'

"Salish, when I think of my talk with the
white stranger, my heart is heavy, and I see only
dark clouds, which hang so low that the mountain-top is buried. For me it matters not. My
trail is short. But for these children and their
children, there is no happy song to lead their
steps.

"Sadness filled my heart. I wandered away
from the stone-house people, and turned my

eyes toward the rising sun. Many people I visited, and then I came to the plains where the buffalo are thick like the blackbirds of autumn. There I met a party of warriors. They were from the north, and had been for many winters on a journey to the far south. These people called themselves Apsaroke. All the Salish know them. With them I traveled far and sang songs with their medicine-men.

"When I reached the land of the north, there I found my brother wanderer. He came from the big waters of the morning sun. His songs are strange, and not like mine. Many stories he can tell you. More than I, he knows about the white men. I will not steal his words.

"The welcome of the Salish has made my old heart young. May I have many winters in your camp. I have said it!"

"Aye, aye, aye, aye!" Like a wave the murmur swept over the assembly as the Clayoquot sat down. Each chief would gladly have leaped to his feet and made a speech, but the second guest must be heard first.

As the latter rose, it could be plainly seen that he was a stranger in the land. His face bore a keener expression. His clothing was different, and instead of a full head of hair with a long braid down each side, he wore but a strip of bristling hair along the crown of his head. His talk was all by signs.

"I am Four Moons. The story of my footsteps on many trails would fill the nights of a long winter. My mother's wigwam was beside the great lakes where streams flow eastward into the Big Water, whence the morning sun rises. My people were the Wendat.[1] Alas! the powerful tribes of the Wendat are broken and scattered.

"Sixty winters ago, in my boyhood days, there

were eighteen great villages of my people. Eight of them were protected by thick, high palisades. The people were like flies in number. Twenty thousand, my father has told me, dwelt in the towns of the Wendat.

Four Moons

"From the earliest time of which the old men could tell, we had been at war with Those of the Long Lodge. Fierce and cruel were the cunning warriors of

[1] The Wendat were a federation of four tribes, nicknamed Hurons by the French. Later they became known as the Wyandot, a corruption of their own name. The Hurons, when first observed by the French explorer Champlain in 1615, were living in what is now Ontario, south and east of Georgian Bay.

Those of the Long Lodge,[1] yet not so numerous as ours.

"I see that you are surprised that the few could overcome the many. But think not that the Wendat were lacking in strength of heart or knowledge of war. Our enemies had help that was not ours.

"Even before I was born there came over the sea in great canoes people of the race about whom my friend has told you. But he has not told you of their wonderful weapons. My friends, when the white hunter would kill a deer, he points a stick at it. There is a flash of lightning, a roar of thunder, and the deer drops dead in his tracks!"

A murmur of awe and wonder, almost of disbelief, swept through the assembly.

[1] This was the native name of the Iroquois, or Five Nations, a federation of the following tribes: Cayuga, Mohawk, Oneida, Onondaga, and Seneca. The territory they occupied is now northern New York. The Iroquois tribes belonged to the same family as the Hurons, the two groups speaking dialects of the same language.

"Yes, my friends, it is true. As the winters passed, the white men in their town beside

the Great Water became more and more numerous. To our enemies, who were nearer to them than we, they traded of these magic weapons for furs. The shooter of the white man will kill ten times as far as an arrow, and when Those of the Long Lodge had many of the new shooters, we could do nothing.

"It is now fifty-two years [1] since they began a war to sweep us from the earth. With their thunder weapons they could not fail. I will not tell you now of the fierce battles, the bloody slaughters, of women wailing for slain husbands and sons, of starving children wandering through the woods.

"A small party fled westward, among them my father, the chief Anabotaha, and myself. I was a young man just learning the ways of war.

"After several years of wandering hither and thither, we came into the country of the Pota-

---

[1] It was in 1648 that the Iroquois began the final campaign against the Huron tribes. In two or three years nearly all the Hurons had been either captured and adopted or killed in battle or by torture. The remnants were scattered in every direction.

watomi[1] and built a village with a palisade on the shore of a great lake so wide that the eye cannot reach across it.

"Still we were not out of reach of Those of the Long Lodge, and a few years later we left this new home. My father, with some others, returned eastward beyond our former land, and later I heard a report that he was killed by our enemies. For my part,

Anabotaha

being now a man, I chose to go with those who continued westward.

"Among the Illinois[2] we found welcome. But our rest here was brief, for the Illinois too were beset by a powerful enemy, the Dakota.[3] And thus, my friends, we were driven from place to

---

[1] In the region of Green Bay, Wisconsin.

[2] The Illinois lived on the river of that name, as well as on the Mississippi.

[3] The Dakota, or Sioux, were living at this early period on the upper course of the Mississippi, above the Illinois. They were very numerous and warlike.

place. With a few companions I became sepa-
rated from the main party, and one by one they
have died. Alone, I have wandered from tribe
to tribe, always westward. As my friend has
told you, it was among the Apsaroke, whom you
know, that he found me.

"You know now, my friends, whence I came.
At another time I will tell you of the habits of
the people of the east. Their ways are strange
to you. I will tell you, too, of the white men,
for I have seen them, and listened to the songs
of their medicine-men, the black-robes,[1] as we of
the east call them. I will show you how on every
seventh day they hold a dance, sing their songs,
and speak to one whom they believe to dwell in
the sky. But now the night is done. For this
time it is enough."

As Four Moons took his seat, a murmur
played over the people gathered there. Then
Lone Pine stood up.

"Salish brothers, the words we have heard tonight bring to my eyes many strange and wonderful pictures. But they make my heart very
sad and heavy, for they show that a new people
with strange words and thoughts are creeping
upon us, and, like old age, nothing can stay
them.

"Sleep is making heavy the eyes of our young
men. Our visitors have promised to stay many
days, and around the council fire to tell us the

[1] The Catholic priests were very commonly called "black-robes."

The return to the lodges

strange things they have heard and seen, and to sing us the songs. We will go to our lodges now."

Late as it was, Kukúsim had kept wide awake to the end. The stories set fire to his blood, and made him want to be a warrior and go on long travels. He decided to take the first opportunity to make friends with these wanderers, particularly with He Who Was Dead And Lives Again, and get them to tell him many stories of their travels, and of the wonders they had seen. The guests slept in his father's lodge, and he lost no part of their talk either in broken words or by signs. In his restless sleep he saw many wonderful sights, and dreamed that he was being carried in a canoe on the swift waters of an angry river, and again and again a hissing snake wound about him.

He was early awake and off to the river with his father and the visitors for the morning bath.

THE SWEAT-BATH

H<small>E</small> W<small>HO</small> W<small>AS</small> D<small>EAD</small> A<small>ND</small> L<small>IVES</small> A<small>GAIN</small> noticed how quick Kukúsim was to understand the hand-talk, and in order to test him he told a story new to the boy, and asked him to repeat it. Quick as a flash the small hands flew back and forth, retelling the story with every detail.

"Good, my grandson! I will be your new grandfather, and I will teach you the ways and wise thoughts of many chiefs and song singers. I will teach you new songs and the ways of many warriors. And when your arm is strong enough to draw the man's bow, your father will know that you are wise and can proudly bear his name."

These words made Kukúsim almost choke with emotion. His thoughts were big.

Scarcely had the sunlight touched the mountain-tops, when Lone Pine called out:

"Brother chiefs, tonight our guests are to talk to us and sing us songs. That these words and songs may do us good and give us strength, let us sing in the sweat-lodge. Thus we shall make the body pure, that the spirit people may come close and take no offense at any human odors."

So after the morning meal a number of men went close to the water's edge, and there made of withes several dome-shaped frames from five

to ten feet in diameter and just high enough
to permit the bathers to squat inside of them.
In the center of each a hole was dug in the
ground, and the frame was then covered with
skins or rush mats. In front of each sweat-lodge
was built a roaring fire, and in it were laid many
stones to heat. When these grew red-hot, a man
took them up one by one with wooden tongs and
placed them in the hole in the center of the sweat-
lodge.

Now the men who were to take part crept into
the low sweat-lodges, and attendants on the outside fastened the covers tightly so that no steam
could escape. The leader in each sweat-lodge
was a medicine-man or a chief, and he had with
him a rattle. When they were all inside, he
started a song, and all the men joined in. At
the end of the fourth song, the head singer took
a cup of water from a vessel before him and
dashed it upon the heated stones. As the hot,
suffocating steam rolled up and filled the little

lodge, the crouching men again commenced to sing. The steam choked them and it was harder now to continue the songs. At the end of that song more water was thrown on; then another song was given.

This continued until songs to the number of four, the sacred number, had been used. At the end of that time the cover was lifted to let in fresh air. After a short breathing space the cover was again lowered, and another series of four songs sung, and again they lifted the cover for air.

Four times the series of four songs was given. One of the men could not endure so much of the heat, and during an interval he went out; but to do that made one look small in the eyes of his people.

At the last song the remainder of the water in the pail was thrown on all at once, which made so much hot steam that it almost overcame even the strongest men. Only one or two of the men could sing to the end of the closing song. At the point when they were almost choked by the heated steam, the covers were lifted, and the bathers ran out and plunged into the icy cold stream. In a moment they were sitting carelessly on the bank, and a little later the sweat was repeated.

Salish boys could not participate with the men in the sweat-lodge. So while the men were preparing their bodies for the story-telling of the night, Kukúsim and his comrades wandered far from the camp, and under a great pine they sat and talked of the wonderful new things they had heard. Kukúsim had understood much more than his companions, so he had much to explain. Rabbit had even gone to sleep during the council, and had heard none of the stories told by the wonderful strangers.

They were all a little jealous of Kukúsim when they found that He Who Was Dead And Lives Again had taken him for a grandson. Scarface was least jealous, for was not Kukúsim his chum?

So great was the excitement and expectancy of this day that the boys neglected to go to their snares, deciding to put that off until another day. When the shadows grew long they returned to camp, and soon they heard the herald calling:

"When it is dark, go to the council lodge! Our friends will tell stories and sing songs. Young men and maidens, put on your fine clothing, that you may dance for the pleasure of our visitors."

From babyhood, even before he could utter words, Kukúsim had been taught by his father to dance, and even at four years of age he had been known as a remarkable dancer. As they sat at the evening meal the old man from the Big Water of the West asked, "Is my grandson to dance for me tonight?" Pleased and happy with this notice, Kukúsim could hardly wait for the meal to end. He was proud of his ability in dancing.

All the family took part in preparing him for the dance. His hair was oiled and combed, his whole body painted red.  Special attention was given his face, which was painted to represent the sky at sunrise—yellow at the chin, and blending through deep colors to a bright crimson at the forehead. In his hair was a bunch of hawk feathers, and on his feet were brown moccasins, and on his legs just below the knees were bands on which were fastened many deer dew-claws. These, when he danced, rattled in rhythm with the songs and drums. Also around his arms were rattles, and at his waist was a scanty loin-cloth of painted deerskin. Besides these things he wore no other clothing.

When all were ready to go to the council lodge, the mother looked proudly at her handsome son.

Kukúsim and his m o t h e r were among the first to r e a c h t h e l o d g e , and they sat watching the others enter. First the proud chiefs stalked in. Nearly all were wrapped with r o b e s of the buffalo, some with the hair outside, others with the smooth skin out and the hair next their bodies. Many of these robes had decorations of gaily colored porcupine quills sewed upon the smooth surface. Others were painted in a way that told the story of the warrior's fasting and battles.

Following the chiefs came the young men. They were prepared for the dance much as was Kukúsim, their bodies painted according to fancy, their hair decorated with feathers. Their blankets they carried on their arms: to wear them would hide from sight their beautifully painted bodies.

Native of west coast

After the young men and warriors came the maids and their mothers, usually in groups of three or four. Girls and boys never went together to public assemblages. While the young men stalked about, wearing only a loin-cloth and a few feathers and proudly displaying their painted and glistening b o d i e s, the maids revealed scarcely so much as an ankle. Their large, loose sleeves fell almost to the wrists. The dresses were decorated with porcupine quills, and on tassels were fastened shells or beads which rattled when they shook. As they entered, the girls and women kept their eyes modestly fixed on the ground.

When all the people were in the council lodge, Lone Pine announced that He Who Was Dead And Lives Again would tell them a story of the land of the West Wind, and then the Salish people would dance to entertain their guests. The wanderer from the west rose.

"Salish, today we have sung together in the

sweat-lodge, and truly we are brothers. When I talk with your old men, I find your words are like those of some of the people beside the Great Water where I spent my boyhood. Soon I shall be able to speak with you without the hand-talk.

"Salish brothers, I have many stories to tell you. Tonight I will begin at the Big Water, where was my father's home.

"My father's house was a frame of great logs covered with planks cut from trees.

A west coast maiden

It was more than half as large as this council lodge. There lived in it many families of our relatives, and they had many slaves. This house, like the others of the village, was near to the water, and on the beach, close in front of the houses, were numerous canoes. These were made of the great trees, and some were so long that they would carry several families. My people knew not the horse, but traveled only in canoes.

The village was on the quiet waters of a bay, but just around a point of wooded land was the Big Water, lashing always in anger against the rock cliffs. Ever we could hear the roar, like constant low thunder; and when the angry winds of winter blew, the water dashed mountain high against the rocks, and no man was brave enough to launch his canoe into the white monster's mouth.

"You would think the dress of my father's people strange. Both men and women wear a blanket made from the bark of cedar trees, but the chiefs and their wives use blankets of smooth-fur animals of the water. When they dance they wear strange masks carved from wood, and they dress themselves with skins, bark, and feathers. The masks represent animals of the kind they see and hunt, and many which do not live but are seen in their dreams. In our dances the maids do not wear beautiful dresses of skin like the Salish, but rather oil their bodies until they glisten in the firelight, and their garment is a short skirt of shredded bark about the hips.

"My heart is sad when I tell you this: at times when the great dances are in progress, men kill slaves and eat them. I hear your words of doubt and of horror at such a story, but my tongue speaks straight, and such is their way. They know no better.

"Fish of many kinds are their food, and the greatest is a monster as big as a hundred buf-

falo. I hear you Salish exclaim 'Oh! Oh!' I know you think my tongue makes large words, but if a whale were placed in this great lodge it would take up more than half its length. To kill this monster in the water is hard work for the men, and only a great chief leads whaling parties. And that he may have success in killing them, he first must spend many weeks alone in the forest, singing and praying that the spirits may make his harpoon go straight, and that the whale may not in anger destroy him and his men.

"When my father was preparing to hunt whales, he lived in the forest for four months, and then sent word to eight men who were his helpers, to go also to the forest and make their bodies pure, that they might have good fortune in capturing a whale. At the appointed time they all came from the woods, got into their great whale canoe, and started far out upon the open water. It was in the springtime, when the whales are not angry. As they started they sang many songs. My father had a hundred whale songs. As they went, my mother and all the women climbed upon the house-tops, singing and beating time on the roof with sticks.

"The spear used by my father was not much longer than his body. Its cutting point was a large mussel-shell held in place with the gum of the pine. The rope fastened to the harpoon was of the bark of the cedar. Fastened to this strong rope were many floats made of air-filled skins of the hair-seal. These floated and dragged in the water, and made the whale tired while he swam or tried to dive.

"The whaling canoe left the smooth bay and

went out into the Great Water. The canoe looked no larger than one's hand.

"Sometimes on the hunt they would not find a whale on the first day, but would have to keep paddling about through the night. In the dark they would hear many whales splashing and

blowing water into the sky. Then when day-light came they might see one close by.

"On sighting a whale they quickly paddled near enough to spear him. If he heard them and sank, they watched closely for him to come to the surface. At last they came near enough to throw harpoons into his body, and as he sank they sang songs to him, praying that he would not be angry. When he came up they harpooned him again, each time fastening more floats to his body.

"Perhaps it would take a whole day to kill a single whale, and when he was dead they had hard work to get him home. When at last they towed him to the village, there was great rejoic-ing; for there would be plenty of food for every one.

"My father was a big chief among his people, as his whale songs were good, and he killed many whales each year.

"At the end of the whale killing my father

often went to visit the Nitinat[1] in the south. When I was almost man grown, he thought he might strengthen his friendship with the proud Nitinat by finding there a wife for me. In ten canoes we started, and on the second day reached the village of the Nitinat. As we came close, our people put on their dance clothing and formed the canoes into a line, with my father's a little ahead. My father had his singers cry out that we had much food and presents, and that the chief was looking for a wife for his son. Then we sang songs of pride and boasting, telling of our courage, our strength, our wealth and rank. The crier shouted:

" 'The great chief, the great whaler, the great warrior would find a wife for his son. His son is strong. His flesh is firm. He has many songs.

[1] The Nĭ'-tĭ-năt formerly lived at the mouth of Jordan River on the southern coast of Vancouver Island. Since the coming of white men they have lived at the mouth of Cheewhat River, near Nitinat Lake.

He buries his rivals with the wealth of his property. He, like his father, will be a great warrior and a great whaler. The girl who becomes his wife must be of a chief's family, must be of good looks, and h e a v y with property.'

"A song of welcome was h e a r d from the shore, and the p r o u d Nitinat weaved into it that their chief was no less great than my father, that all the women of royal blood were beautiful to look at, and no one could outdo them in gifts. Great was our welcome, and great the feasting. Soon a maid was selected for me, and after the next whaling season her people would return the visit and bring her with the wedding presents.

"But the winds of the ocean had another story. Our singers and wise men had grown too proud to listen to the voice of the medicine-man of the Nitinat. With black-painted face he came from the forest, waving his arms and closing his eyes, exclaiming: 'I see dark clouds, heavy clouds, angry clouds! I hear war upon the waves, and cries of anger, and I see blood upon the water!'

"'He sings these gloomy songs that we may give him presents,' protested our medicine singers. 'No disaster can befall our great chief.'

"Homeward bound we put into a bay for protection from a threatening storm. There we watched for the angry ocean to calm, yet fury worse than the angry ocean was near by, and we saw it not. In a cove forming a part of the bay in which we had found shelter, there lay concealed more than a hundred war canoes of the hated Clallam.[1] They had seen us enter, and their spies came close upon our camp.

"'At tomorrow's dawn we will renew our homeward journey,' said my father.

"In the darkness our old men fancied they heard strange sounds. And well they might have, for when the darkness lifted, there upon the water, completely blocking the mouth of the bay, were the countless canoes of the enemy. Flight to the forest was suggested, but no words were needed to tell us that the enemy was as thick in the woods as on the water.

[1] The Clallam were a warlike people living in a dozen stockaded villages on the south side of the Strait of Juan de Fuca, in what is now the State of Washington.

"Then my father sang his war song and shouted: 'No more shall we see our home! Let our fighting be worthy our name!'

"Spears and clubs were made ready as the medicine-men sang their songs, and then our handful of canoes, close grouped, rushed in attack upon the enemy.

"Salish, never again in my life shall I see such fighting. It was ten canoes of the enemy to one of our own. This was no fighting with bows and arrows, but with spears and clubs and knives. Canoes were capsized, and the fight continued in the water. The way of that land is to take the head of the slain enemy. A score of canoes circled about my father, and furious was the fighting as he beat the enemy back. And then the blow of a heavy club threw him into the water.

"Many of our women were taken for slaves, and some of our young men. I was made as if dead with the stroke of a club, and when I came

The snow mountains

to life I found myself tightly bound in the bottom of a canoe, along with other captives and a pile of gory heads. Angry warriors who had lost friends would have killed us, but our masters would not give up their slaves.

"Half a day we traveled south to the home of the Clallam. Their village, like ours, was close to the water, but their houses were smaller, and they had no carved posts or dance masks. Their village was on small, quiet waters far from the open ocean. You have seen nothing like that land or its ways. All the heads of our people taken by the Clallam were stuck on the tops of poles in front of their houses.

"My heart was always heavy, and I waited for a time when I could steal a canoe and return to my home-land. My owner saw the thoughts in

A dancing scene

my heart, and took me to Nisqualli [1] and there traded me to people who lived far from the water, eastward across the snow mountains.

"My heart was sick in this strange land. The air was dry and hot. The great treeless plains burned under the scorching sun. I constantly longed for my father's home-land by the Great Water, and the cool shadows of its forests. The food of a slave was bitter in the mouth of one who was the son of a great chief.

"Salish, I have told you the story of my youth. Now I would see your young men and women dance. I will rest."

Lone Pine rose to his feet.

[1] Nisqualli is an extensive prairie at the head of Puget Sound, through which flows Nisqualli River. This region, the home of the Nisqualli tribe, was visited every autumn by Indians from near and far, to gather acorns and to trade.

Young men dancing

"Salish, the words of He Who Was Dead And Lives Again are wonderful. We cannot understand the fish as big as a hundred buffalo. We thought the man-size fish, the sturgeon, taken from the great river, was the largest of fish. And when he tells us of men eating the bodies of other men, our hearts are sick and we are glad we do not have such evil ways. Great was the story of our friend.

"Now, young men, you will dance. Let us see how strong are your legs. The old men and women will feel young again. When it is your time to dance, be happy, and show our visitors that the eyes of the Salish are as bright as any in the land."

Far into the night lasted the dancing. At times the young men performed alone, at times in company with the maids. Furious was the dancing of the old chiefs and warriors, as they acted in pantomime the story of their battles.

Kukúsim danced alone, with every eye upon his supple movements, and no one shouted louder approval than his new grandfather.   His happy smile told Kukúsim that he had a real place in the heart of the old man.

HE WHO MADE ALL THINGS FIRST

On the day after the dance a big thought came to Kukúsim.

"Grandfather," he said, "will you go with Scarface and me to our traps, and in the forest perhaps tell us a story?"

"My son, you should not have so bold a heart," said his mother, reprovingly.

"Scold not!" said the old man. "My heart was empty, and I have taken him for my grandson. Not wishing to be selfish in his pleasures, Kukúsim has asked to have Scarface with him. That is good. I shall have two grandsons."

Soon they were away to the forest, the broad-shouldered man and the two boys. As the trail approached a deep, quiet pool in the river, Kukúsim whispered, "Here lives the Father Fish of the river."

They stood quietly and looked into the clear water, and far below lay the monster. His body was nearly as long as that of Kukúsim.

"Some day I will show my grandson how to catch that fish," promised the Clayoquot.

A blue jay perched on a high limb shook his head and scolded, and a kingfisher dived into the water and came up with a small fish.

"I will tell sometime the story of how the blue jay got his topknot," went on the old man. "That topknot was once his war-club."

"Listen, Grandfather. Hear the drumming of the partridge! Do you know a story of that?"

"Come close, my Grandsons, that I may tell you a great secret."

They nestled close to him, and he put his arms about them.

"Yes, Grandsons, the partridge has a story. The squirrel which sits

Kukúsim's mother

on yonder limb and scolds our presence has a story. Do you see that tiny insect crawling on the ground? It too has a story. See that great pine with its roots drawing life from the earth, our Mother, and its branches reaching out to the sky, our Father, and that slender blade of grass growing at its roots. Each, my Grandsons, has its own story. Look! Do you see that tiny speck against the clouds? That is a pelican. See that tiny bird flashing from flower to flower. And there is a monster bird which men see only in visions. All have their stories."

In wide-eyed wonder Kukúsim asked, "Grand-father, can you tell all those stories?"

"The sun is looking at us through the trees. Each day it comes out of the east and travels to the west, and never grows tired. Some of the people say the sun is the Great Father, and sees all the animals, birds, insects, trees, fish, and plants, and knows their stories. Others say the sun is only the scout of the One Who Knows All, and is sent out each day to do his work, to give light, to give warmth, to make happy the people. The Apsaroke call this powerful person I-tsík-ba-dish, which means He Who Made All Things First. They say that he made all things, does all things, hears all things, sees all things."

"I-tsík-ba-dish," repeated the two boys, "He Who Made All Things First." Wider grew their eyes with wonder.

"Does he hear that squirrel talking to us? Does he see that little flower? Does he know the little stone which I took from the water's edge?"

"Yes, my Grandsons, the Apsaroke think so."

"Then, Grandfather, he sees us sitting here, and hears our words. If we walk and talk in the dark, does he see us and know our thoughts?"

"Yes, my Grandsons."

So big was the idea, that long were the boys speechless. Many thoughts came to Kukúsim, and his mind was full of questions.

Each day the sun starts upon its journey

"Grandfather, last night you told of the great fish killed by your father. A fish so large must have a great story. Could you tell us that?"

"Yes, the whale has a story, and soon you shall hear it. But, my Grandson, sometimes the smaller animal has a bigger story than the large one. Perhaps the reason of that is that the smaller animal thinks more. In my father's land the little mink has a story bigger than the whale's story."

"We know the mink. We often see him playing by the river, and once I caught one in a trap. Grandfather, let us go and look at the rabbit snares."

They found the first one just as they had left it. No rabbit had been that way. Then came a thought to Kukúsim.

"Perhaps I-tsík-ba-dish told the rabbit about that trap, and he kept away."

"My Grandsons, I do not think it was I-tsík-ba-dish; but the rabbit which was caught before and made his escape told his brothers, and they all kept away from this trail."

Soon they reached the swamp where the bear had been seen, and the boys told their new grandfather of the mother and the baby bear; but they did not tell him how frightened they had been. However, he had been a boy once, and knew.

"When the bear snorted and ran, my boys felt weak in the knees, I think."

"How did you know that, Grandfather?"

"Old men know a great deal, my Grandsons."

"Then I-tsík-ba-dish, who knows all things, must be very old, Grandfather."

"Yes, Grandsons, he is old. The Piegan call this person Nápiw, which means Old Man."

"Grandfather," laughed Scarface, "you know so many things that we should call you Nápiw."

At the second snare they found a rabbit held high by the noose. The boys shouted with glee and thought of what a fine supper it would make.

Lonely travelers

The men wore skins of strange animals

The third snare was sprung, and empty.

"Perhaps that was a mother rabbit," suggested Kukúsim, "and her baby needed her. I am not sorry that the snare did not hold her.

"Grandfather, you have not told us a real story yet. Let us sit here under the pine, while you tell about some of the animals."

The old man did not speak for a long time. He closed his eyes and leaned back against the tree trunk, and the boys knew he was seeing many things.

"My Grandsons, as your fathers have told you, there was a time when all the animals and men were alike, and the old men say they all talked together. The animals could lay off their skins and feathers like shirts, and go about like human beings. Then came a time when men spoke different words, and did not wear skins like the bear, the wolf, and the cougar, or feathers like the eagle and the goose. I will tell of the time

when men and animals were one, the long ago stories. The first will be a tale related by the people living at the mouth of the Big River in the west [Columbia], and is of the time when an evil creature was destroying the people."

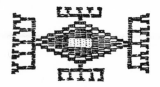

"At the mouth of the Great River lived an ogress. She would tie a captive upon a cradle-board and send it adrift into the fog with the command, 'Go forever!' After a while the board would come floating back to her out of the fog, with nothing but bones on it. For it had been to a place of such great heat that the flesh had been melted from the bones.

"On the sandy beach sat many people await-ing their turn. The magic of the ogress made them unable to run away.

"Then came Coyote, who in those days looked like a man.

"He said, 'I will try that, and soon I shall return.'

"So he was tied to the board, and as he floated away the ugly old woman cried, 'Go forever!' But the people shouted, 'Come back again!'

"The board disappeared, but after a long time it was seen again coming ashore with Coyote still tied fast, unhurt. He was too strong for the magic of the ogress.

"Wishing to show that she was just as strong, the old woman now allowed Coyote to bind her to the cradle-board, and as she went drifting out into the fog, all the captive people joined Coyote in the shout, 'Go forever!' In time the board came back with nothing but her white bones on it. And so the people were saved from this evil being.

"Coyote then went up the river bank to a place where two women had all the salmon penned in

a pond. He saw the women in a canoe gathering driftwood for fuel, and he changed himself into a piece of wood and floated down the stream. He wished them to take him, so that he might free the salmon; but they let him drift by. Then he went back above the place

Coyote went up the river

and changed himself into a baby on a cradle-board. When the crying baby floated near the canoe, one of the women drew it out of the water and took it home to care for it. They gave the child a piece of dried eel to suck, and it fell asleep.

"In the morning they gave him another piece of eel and went out to gather more wood. As soon as they were gone, Coyote untied the cords that fastened him to the cradle-board and turned himself back into a man. He took five sharp

Letting out the salmon

oak sticks which the women used for digging roots, and ran to the pond where the salmon were. Only a narrow piece of land was between the pond and the great river. Coyote began to dig away the earth as fast as he could. When one stick was broken he took another and dug away. He was using his fifth digger when the women saw what he was doing.

" 'Oh,' cried the elder sister, 'we shall lose all our fine fish, and then we shall have nothing to eat but roots!'

"They paddled swiftly toward Coyote, but just as the canoe reached the shore, he pried off the last mass of earth. Water began to pour out of the pond into the river, and the salmon were carried with it.

"Coyote picked up a lump of white clay and ran toward the two sisters.

" 'It is not right for you to have all these fish penned up!' he cried.

"He threw the piece of clay and it struck the younger sister on the forehead, leaving a white mark. He did the same to the other, and then said:

" 'You two shall be swallows, and shall be seen at salmon time.'

"And the two women were turned into birds, and flew away. And now, each year when the salmon come, many swallows are seen building their nests in the rocks. The salmon swam up the Great River, and since then all the people on its banks and on the streams that flow into it have had salmon for food.

"Farther up the river Coyote saw a canoe in midstream. Soon the head of a man came up near the canoe, and the man had a large fish under each arm. He threw them into the boat, and dived for more.

"This was very strange. A man catching fish by diving! While the man was under the water, Coyote swam out and took one of the fish. Then he hid behind a large oak and watched. The diver came up again and counted his fish. He climbed into his canoe and sat there looking at them. Soon he pointed his finger straight up at the sky and moved it in a circle. At last, when the finger pointed directly at the oak, it stopped.

"In great fear Coyote dodged, but the finger kept following him. Then the fisherman paddled ashore, and Coyote saw that he had no mouth.

The strange man walked toward Coyote, all the time pointing his finger. He could not speak, and Coyote thought that this was his way of blaming him for stealing the fish.

"Then Coyote gathered some stones, built a fire, and cooked the fish on the hot stones. He gave a piece to the stranger, who smelled it and threw it away. Coyote thought for a moment, then took a sharp piece of stone, felt the fisherman's face, and suddenly cut a straight slit where the mouth should be.

" 'Be quick and wash your face!' he cried.

"When the man had washed off the blood, he ate the fish and said, 'My friend, you should have cooked a larger fish.'

A girl of the Columbia River

" 'Why,' said Coyote, 'you nearly poked out my eye for taking this small one!'

"The man now led Coyote to his village, where all the people were without mouths. Coyote made mouths for all of them, but he cut them a little too large. That is why the people of that village to this day have larger mouths than others, and talk more loudly.

"At another place Coyote saw a man turning somersaults, landing on his head and yelling loudly as if it hurt him. Wondering what this meant, Coyote went closer and found that the man had his ankles tied and between his legs a bundle of firewood.

" 'What is the matter, my friend?' asked Coyote.

" 'There is nothing the matter,' answered the man. 'I am carrying this firewood to my house.'

" 'But that is no way to carry wood,' said Coyote.

"He untied the man's legs, cut some withes, twisted them into a rope, and attached it to the bundle of wood. Then he swung the fagot to his back, passing the loop of the rope across his forehead, and so he carried it for the man. Thus the people of that village first learned the use of the pack-strap.

"After a while Coyote in his travels came to a stream [White Salmon River] flowing into the Great River. Here was a very large village.

As he sat on the bank he said, 'I wish some young person would get me a drink of water.'

" A woman answered: 'Nobody here drinks water. We have a hard time to get it.'

"He asked what was the trouble, and in order to show him a young girl was sent with a pail. Coyote carefully watched her. She waded into the stream and began to dip up water. Suddenly she dropped the vessel, screamed, and ran away. Another girl was sent for water, and she behaved in the same way. Then Coyote himself waded into the stream at the same spot and dipped a pail full of water. He saw two white salmon chasing each other in fun

with mouths wide open. 'This is what these foolish people fear,' he said to himself.

"When he brought the water, a great crowd of thirsty people ran to him. He carried water until all were satisfied. Then Coyote went into the woods and cut some long poles and gathered some long strings of bark. With these he made spears, and then taught the people of this village how to spear salmon and cook them on hot stones.

Carrying with pack-strap

"Coyote's next adventure was with an ogress and Owl, her husband. These two evil creatures would catch people, roast them in a pit, and eat them. Coyote thought for a long time how he might overcome them. Then he cut some green fir cones into bits and dried them. He placed them on strings like beads, and tied the strings around his legs, arms, and neck, in many close rows. Then he covered himself with a robe and went to the home of the ogress.

"She came out to meet him and asked, 'Where are you going?'

"He answered: 'You see where the sun comes out in the morning? That is where I am going. My wife died a few days ago and I feel sad and do not wish to remain at home. She was a good wife. So I do not like to talk to women yet.'

"He began to dance, and the dry cones under his robe rattled. The ogress ran up to take him by the arm, but he dodged.

"She asked, 'How did you become so that you could make that sound when you dance?'

" 'You need not ask that,' he replied, 'because I would not tell you, no matter how much you might pay me. If I told you that, you would never have to hunt for food, but only dance thus  and the people would come to you. Then you would have only the work of cooking them.'

"He started as if to leave her, but she came up with him again and begged to know how he made that sound. He pretended that he did not wish to tell, but at last he agreed to give her the secret.

The Ogress

"Said he: 'It is my bones that rattle when I dance. I had my body covered with pitch, eyes and all. Then I was put on the fire. The pitch burned over my skin, and my bones were roasted dry. That is why they rattle, because they are dry and charred. Hear my head!' and he shook it. 'Hear my legs!' and he shook them.

" 'Good!' said the ogress. 'I am glad to know this, and I shall do it. Let us go up and you can work on me.'

"She led him up to the pit where she cooked the captured people. All around the edge of this

The Witch's cooking pit

great hole sat her captives, old and young, waiting for their turn to be roasted. All were weeping, and around the pit were piles of bones.

"Coyote sent some of the prisoners into the woods for pitch, and soon they brought what was needed. A great fire was built, and Coyote covered the body of the ogress thickly with pitch. Then he pushed her into the fire, and at once she began to blaze. Coyote quickly gave each of five men a forked pole, one to hold her down by the neck, the others by the legs and arms. Whenever Coyote ordered her to be turned, they rolled her over. In a short time the creature was dead, and Coyote sent the people to their homes.

"Soon Coyote saw Owl, the husband, coming home with a great number of prisoners. He threw a handful of ashes at Owl, and said: 'This is not the way to do. It is wrong to roast these people. There is going to be another kind of people here, and this must stop. I have killed

On the banks of the Columbia

your wife because she did this. From now on you shall be nothing but a bird, and your name shall be Owl, and you shall live among these rocks. Once in a great while your voice shall be heard, and then some one will die.'

"As Coyote finished speaking, Owl was changed into a bird, and his feathers were gray because of the ashes.

"So Coyote traveled far and wide, changing evil beings into harmless things. Sometimes he made mistakes; but all things as they are now, good or bad, were made so by Coyote."

A satisfied sigh came from the two boys. "Truly, a wonderful person was Coyote!" exclaimed Kukúsim.

"And truly, foolish were the people in those days," said Scarface. "Did they know nothing of the ways we have?"

"That was long, long ago," explained the old man, "and they had not yet learned. Knowl-

edge comes slowly. Men with great hearts find new and better ways, and Coyote, I suppose, was one of those great ones."

FOUR MOONS TELLS ABOUT THE MANDAN

The sun was low when the old man and his boy companions reached the camp. The herald was going about the encampment announcing the council of the evening, and they stopped to listen.

"Salish, tonight we are to gather again in the council lodge. This night Four Moons will tell us of things he has seen on his long travels. Young men and women, dress for the dance! Let us dance that our hearts may be glad!"

As they came to the chief's lodge, Kukúsim's mother gently chided the boys: "You were gone so long that I thought perhaps the Thunder Birds [1] had stolen you."

"No, Mother, we did not see the Thunder

[1] Many Indian tribes believe that in the sky live huge birds, the flash of whose eyes causes the lightning and the flapping of whose wings, the thunder.

Birds, but I learned many strange things, and when I am a man I am going to travel far to see them for myself. I shall take Scarface with me."

"When you have grown to be a man you will have a wife, and she will see that you go each day to hunt and fish, that there may be food in the lodge. Little time will you have to wander in strange lands when you have a wife to feed."

"No, Mother, I shall take no wife until I am an old man. Meanwhile I shall be a warrior, a singer, and a wanderer."

"Eat your food, and prattle not of wandering. It was but yesterday you were a babe at my breast. You are not yet a man."

Soon the people were again in the long lodge for an evening of stories and merry-making. After the smoke Lone Pine rose to his feet and said:

"Last night we were told of the land where the sun goes to sleep. Tonight the one who came from the land of the new day will talk to us. Our friend Four Moons will speak. I have said it."

The earth lodge

Four Moons slowly rose, looked about over his audience, and in the sign language began his speech.

"Salish, I am more a stranger to you than He Who Was Dead And Lives Again, as I speak no word of your tongue. So with my hands alone I must tell my story.

"Last night our friend from the western water spoke of the home of his father. The trail to my father's home is so long that tonight I see it only as through a heavy fog. I will think much, and another night the trail will be clearer. To-night I will tell you of a people closer to you.

"They live in the center of the country where feed so many of the buffalo, and they are called the People of the Earth-covered Houses.[1] Their villages are beside a big river. Its waters are

[1] Many tribes applied this name to the Mandan, who lived in several fortified villages of hemispherical houses on the Missouri River, in what is now North Dakota. The Mandan, who are now nearly extinct, are related to the Sioux, although they never were friendly with them. The traditions of the Mandan indicate that they once lived on the Gulf of Mexico near the mouth of the Mississippi.

not clear like the stream we now hear flowing swiftly through the forest, but thick with mud, and of the color of the ripened prairie grass. They live not in houses of skins, blankets, or rushes, but in structures built of logs covered with earth—cool in summer, warm in winter. They kill many buffalo, yet do not have only that food. They have fields where they raise corn and squashes, as did my father's people.

"They sing songs and make prayers, the words of which, they say, cause the game to be plentiful; and they sing and pray to the spirits who care for the crops, for it is most important that the corn grow and ripen well.

"The stories of long ago say that these people traveled far to reach this home-land. In the beginning they lived far away in the south, where the sun ever shines and the birds always sing. For the period of many lives they traveled, always up the great river. When they find it necessary to cross this stream they use a boat which would bring a laugh to the face of our friend from the western water. It is small and round,

like one of your horn dishes, and will carry but two people. It is made by stretching fresh buffalo skins over a framework of willows. They told me of a war party that used more than a hundred of these.

"The strangest thing about the People of the Earth-covered Lodges is their great dance.

"In the beginning of the world, they say, there was but one man on the earth, and the name by which they call him is One Man. The ground was not yet hardened, and in order not to break through the crust he had to run quickly. He it was who created rivers, lakes, springs, hills, and trees, making the earth ready for the people who were to come.

"As he ran about the land, One Man was always looking for other beings like himself. At last he decided to make some.

"At the place where the river flows into the Great Water far away in the south, he took the lower rib from each side of his body. Of the right he formed a man, and of the left a woman. He left them together, and when he returned he found they had two children, a boy and a girl.

Turtles that look like islands

He lifted the children up into the air and sang, and thus caused them to become at once man and woman. In the same way three more men and women were created.

"There were now five pairs of human beings, and these were the beginning of the five villages of the People of the Earth-covered Lodges. So say the old men.

"After many years One Man again came back from his wanderings over the earth, and lived among them. He began to wonder what he could do to help the people become strong. He decided, with the aid of Black Eagle, a magician, to teach them a new dance, which would cause the spirits to favor them.

"Eight buffalo masks were made, and for the drum they tried Badger. But one blow of the drumstick drove his legs into the ground, strong as he was.

"Then they asked Beaver to be the drum, but

he said: 'I am soft, for I live in the mud. If Badger was not good, I surely would not do.'

"In his search for some animal to be the drum, One Man came to the Great Water. Having magic power, he walked far out on the water. In the distance he saw what seemed to be a clump of weeds; but going closer he found it to be large oaks growing from the cracks in the shells of four huge Turtles. The Turtles were like islands; their shells were like rough rocks of many colors.

" 'My friends,' said One Man, 'I am looking for a drum. My people have fine corn and good food, and I beg you to go with me.'

"Said they: 'We are just like land in this place. We are very heavy. But if you can take us we will go.'

"One Man stretched out his magic staff and made the water walk back. He stooped to lift the Turtles, but they were much too heavy.

Turtle-Drums

" 'Look well at our bodies,' they said to him; 'then go home and make buffalo-skin shells just like ours, and we will go into them.'

"So One Man went home, and with thick buffalo-skin he made four drums, which looked just like the great Turtles. And the spirits of the

The Mandan dance

Turtles entered them, and have been there ever since. Then One Man called the people together, and taught them the new dance.

"My friends, I have seen that dance. Truly, it is a dance for strong men. It takes place in a big, dirt-covered lodge, and it lasts four days. In the evening of the first day all the young men who wish to have visions and thus obtain the aid of the spirits come slowly into the lodge. For three days and three nights they stay in the dance lodge without food or water. Only a strong heart can do that. But that is not all.

"The days and nights are spent in singing and dancing. The singers squat on the ground beside the buffalo-skin drums and beat on them, and while they sing the others dance. Some are dressed like buffalo, some like bears, some like eagles, and many like other beasts and birds.

"At the close of the third day comes the great thing. To each one of the young men who have

been fasting comes a man with a knife. He raises
the flesh on the young man's breast and pushes
the point of the knife through it, making a slit
in the flesh. Then he does the same thing on the
other breast.

"Next he pushes a round stick through each
slit, and over each stick he fastens a loop in the
end of a long rope. The rope is then thrown up
over a beam high above the ground, and the
dancers pull on it until the young man is jerked
off his feet. There he hangs, swinging in the air,
and the blood drips from his wounds.

"Think not, Salish, that this is cruelty. It is
the religion of these people. When from hunger

CHEYENNE SUN-DANCE SONG

and suffering the young man faints, he is lowered to the ground. As he lies there, he has a

vision. The spirits come and speak to him, and teach him songs which will give him strength throughout his life. This is their way, and they believe that so long as it is followed they will be a powerful nation.

"That is the end."

At the morning meal Kukúsim was thinking of the big fish in the pool, which his new grandfather had promised to catch for them. The Clayoquot saw his thoughtful eyes, and asked, "What is it, my Grandson?"

"You promised to help me catch the big fish. Let us do it today."

"So be it, Grandson. Get Scarface, and we will go after him."

Leaning against the back of the lodge was a long pole with a wide prong at one end. Over the two forks was stretched the mouth of a mesh bag. This was Lone Pine's dip-net.

As a rule the dip-net was used only in taking salmon from the eddies of large streams, but the great char in the deep pool was worthy of the net.

There was no need to caution Kukúsim and Scarface not to show themselves to the fish. Almost on their stomachs they crept to the edge of the overhanging bank, and not a blade of grass was shaken as their black eyes peered over. Far below like a dim shadow they saw the monster's form.

"Slowly, very slowly," murmured the old man, as he pushed the net into the water some distance behind the char. When it was at the right depth he carefully pushed it forward, inch by inch, until the great body was almost enclosed by the net. Then at the instant of releasing the string which held its mouth spread open, he gave a powerful forward sweep with the pole. The mouth of the net closed the moment the string was let go, and the fish was safely caught.

When the glistening creature lay on the grass, the boys fell upon the leaping, threshing body, and with arms and knees held it fast while the old man killed it by striking its head with a stick.

"Now that we have the big fish," begged Kukú-sim, when their prize lay lifeless, "tell us a story of your father's home, where the monster fish is."

As they sat under the pines beside the rushing stream, the Clayoquot said:

"When I talked in council, I spoke of the big house of my father's people. Now I will tell you how they make these homes.

"With tools of stone and hard wood men go into the forest and cut down many large trees.

The first ones are for the four great posts. In cutting down the trees they use a stone maul to drive the stone-pointed chisel into the wood, and thus pry off great chips. When the tree is down, they cut off a piece long enough for a post. Then with the same tools they make it into the shape wanted.

"Now a man begins with small chisels to carve all sorts of figures on these posts, — whales, wolves, bears, eagles. These images tell the story of the origin of the names of those who are to live in that house.

"On one of my father's house posts was carved a great bear, because, so they say, in the time when animals could throw off their skins and be men, his first ancestor was a bear. In the bear's mouth was a human body which the bear seemed to be devouring. This was to record the fact that my father once killed a slave in order to show the people that his wealth was so great he could afford to kill a valuable slave.

"From other logs the workmen now split wide planks to cover the house. When a plank is first split it is too rough to use, and with small tools

they smooth it. All this is hard work and requires much time. It takes a number of men all of one summer to make planks enough for a single house.

"When the posts and planks are put in place to form the house, there is a great feast, and many presents are given away and great speeches made."

"In our camp," said the boys, "our mothers prepare all the skins and make the lodges. Do not the mothers in your village help to make the houses?"

"No, that is not their part of the work. The men build the houses, the women only take care of them and the things in them."

"Do the men make the canoes, too?"

"Yes. No woman would know how to make a canoe. Men fell one of the forest's largest trees, and with stone mauls and chisels slowly hollow it out. Sometimes they use fire to help in this. Then, when it is roughly shaped, they put away

Shooting salmon

their mauls and chisels, and take small hand chisels, and with these chip, chip, chip away for day after day until at last the canoe is almost ready for the water.

"To give it a final smoothing they use firebrands of long cedar splints. These they hold close to the surface of the wood until it is slightly charred, and keep moving them along. The charred surface is then rubbed off with a rough stone, and finally smoothed with a bunch of cedar bark worked into soft fiber."

"What do your people eat besides the flesh of the whale?"

"We have many kinds of fish which are caught in different ways, and plenty of clams, large and small. And there are the sea-lion and the seal."

Instantly the boys wanted to know how these animals were caught and killed.

"The hair-seal," their teacher explained, "lives in the Great Water, and his food is fish. When the sun shines he lies sleeping on the rocks, basking in its warmth. The people of the land where I was born are very fond of the flesh of the hair-

Harpooning seal

seal, and this is one of their ways of killing him. Many times have I watched my father.

"He used a spear more than three times the height of a man, and to its point was fastened a strong line thirty times as long as the reach of a man's two arms. The other end of this line was tied about his waist.

"After removing his fur robe, my father would slip into the water. He would float under the surface with nothing but his face and the top of his head showing, and his long hair made him look very much like a swimming seal. Thus he would swim toward the basking hair-seals.

"When he was close to them and in shallow water, he would suddenly rush forward and throw the long spear into one of them. Then he would quickly run back to the shore and brace his heels in the sand to hold the seal from escaping into the water. If the animal was a small one he had no trouble, but sometimes a very large male would break the line and dive into the water, carrying the spear with him.

"When the seal was tired out with fighting and bleeding, my father would run down and club him on the head. Then he would take out the spear point and stop up the wound with a plug of grass or a piece of wood. This was to keep the blood from running out, for they are very fond of the blood.

"We cooked the seal in this way. Two small logs are laid close beside each other, and a fire is built between them. The seal is placed on the logs over the flames and is rolled over and over until all the hair is burned off. Then the crisp skin is scraped clean with a shell.

"The thick fat which covers the body of a seal is cut off in strips, which are boiled in water. As the oil rises to the surface of the water, it is skimmed off with large shells and poured into the clean, dry stomach of another seal. This oil my people eat with dried berries and with cooked meat.

"The flesh of the seal is boiled with the blood. My people boil meat as do yours, by heating water with red-hot stones. Only, instead of the water-tight baskets which you have, the vessel used is made with wide strips of wood.

"*Ha ho!* This talk of the land and the food of my youth makes me long for a feast on the fat flesh of the hair-seal. But perhaps it would not taste so good to me now that I have become used to the juicy meat of the buffalo and the antelope.

"Let us now go home, that your mother may have the fish for our evening meal."

THE SNAKE DANCE

GLAD was Kukúsim's mother to have so fine a
fish. Some of it she broiled by slicing off large
steaks, holding them flat with skewers, and
placing each piece in the cleft end of a stick thrust
into the ground beside the fire. The remainder
she boiled in water which she had heated in a
skin vessel by dropping red-hot stones into it
until it bubbled.

As they ate their evening meal, Kukúsim's
mother asked: "What new and wonderful things
did you learn today? If you spend many days
with our guest you will know more than Seven
Stars, the story teller. I know he is already
jealous of you."

"Soon my grandfather is to teach me songs."

"Soon you are to go to the mountains and
look for songs for yourself. Your father and
Seven Stars have already talked of your going."

Such warning words he had often heard, and
knew that before many moons had passed he,
like other boys, must go into the lonely places,
looking for spiritual power. Even now he could
hear his father and the Clayoquot talking of
many good things which had come to them
through their fasting.

While they were still eating, the herald was
riding about the camp, calling out: "Tonight He
Who Was Dead And Lives Again will tell us
more about his travels, and again we shall dance.
Let us dance well tonight, for our chief, Lone

Pine, and his counselors have talked long today, and soon we shall cross the mountains to the buffalo country."

At the word "buffalo" Kukúsim grew excited.

"Father, am I not big enough for the hunt?"

"Winters must pass yet before you will be strong enough to draw the buffalo bow, which buries the arrow's point in the heart."

Then a thought that hurt him came to Kukúsim, and at the first opportunity he slipped close to the Clayoquot

Seven Stars

and in a low voice asked, "Do you go to the buffalo land?"

"Yes, Grandson, I shall take some of the horses your father gave me, and go with your party. Perhaps your mother will let you ride one of my horses."

As they drew near the council lodge, they could plainly hear the drums and singing. Six

or eight young men were sitting on the ground about a big d r u m . Some were b e a t i n g it, and all were singing. When the chief came in they stopped and remained quiet, waiting for the dancing to begin.

"This is our last n i g h t to dance and hear stories in t h i s l o d g e ," said Lone Pine when all had assembled. "Today we have counseled, and after one more day we shall start for the land of the buffalo. For more than two moons our men have been making r e a d y their bows, arrows, and knives, and the women have made many moccasins. Well must we be prepared, as we go into the land of the enemy, and they may war upon us.

"Our guests who have traveled so far will come with us upon the hunt, and we hope they will return with us, that we may spend the long nights of winter around the council fire. They know much that will help to make our nation strong. Tonight He Who Was Dead And Lives Again will tell us of strange tribes he has seen. I have said it."

A Hopi maiden

"Salish," said their guest, speaking now in their own language but using his hands to assist him, "last night Four Moons told you of the People of the Earth-covered Lodges, who raise corn and squashes.

"Now I will tell you of another tribe who raise corn. They are the people of the stone houses and the Snakes. They call themselves the Hopi.[1] Their villages are in the midst of the land of sand. They have no river or lakes, and the rains seldom come. That is the reason they sing songs to the Snakes, for it is believed they bring the rain.

"The Hopi villages are on the top of high cliffs; the housetops seem to touch the blue sky.

[1] The Hopi, frequently called the Moqui, still live in several villages of stone houses in northeastern Arizona.

Going into the desert for snakes

There they build them, that they may easily protect their women and children and stores of corn from the warring Navaho, Apache, and Ute. They build the walls of their homes thick with heavy stones. The entrance is through the roof, that they may better protect themselves from the enemy. To enter they climb to the top of the house on a ladder, and then descend another to the room below. At nightfall, and in times of attack, the outside ladders are drawn up to the housetop.

"The wives and maidens of the Hopi have soft voices, and make glad the eye with their bright faces and happy smiles.

"For many winters I tarried in the land of the Hopi. Their singing men have much knowledge. Their songs are great with power, and their dancing brings the rain-clouds low. Long was I with them before they would call me brother and let me join my voice with theirs to the Snakes.

"Important are the Four Winds to the Hopi, and when they go to the desert for the Snakes they go first to the land of the North Wind. Then on the next day they go to the land of the West Wind, another day to the land of the South Wind, and on the fourth day to the land of the East Wind.

"The Hopi call the Snakes brothers, and would not in any way harm them.

"Before going out upon the sand waste to find the Snakes, the men of the Snake brotherhood spend days in an underground room, singing songs, and praying to the Snakes."

Every listener sat in wide-eyed wonder. Certainly this was strange medicine. Kukúsim, sitting close to Scarface, thought of many things he would ask Grandfather.

"Then on a day when all are ready they begin the search for the brother Snakes. When the men come to the foot of the stone cliffs, they stop at a spring which bubbles from the foot of the rocks. There they make prayers, and scatter meal of the corn upon the water.

Snake dance

"When these songs and prayers are over, they begin to walk across the sands, looking for the Snakes. When one is found, they gather about it and make a prayer. At its close one of them scatters meal on the Snake. Then with a quick motion he picks it up in the right hand, passing it to the left and holding its head toward the Sun.

"Now, Salish, listen! It is the Snake That Rattles, the bite of which brings death. But the Hopi knows the secret, and has no fear, and with meal in his hand he strokes the head of the Snake four times."

"Ah! Ah!" murmured the Salish. "Truly, that is great medicine!"

The Clayoquot continued: "He now puts the Snake into a leather carrying-sack, and again they take up the search, and all through the day it is thus. Then, when the sun has gone to sleep in the west, they return to the underground room, which they call *kíva* [kē'-va]. There they sing songs, and place the Snakes in earthen jars. For four days they capture Snakes in this way.

"Many of the Snake brotherhood are not fully grown. I have seen among them boys not so old as Kukúsim, the chief's son."

"I am glad I am not a Hopi!" thought the boy,

A snake priest

shuddering at the story he had heard.

"On the ninth day of this great ceremony they dance with the Snakes. This occurs in an open place in the village, where all the people can see. At noon of that day they purify the Snakes by washing them in a large earthen jar of water. While they wash them, they sing songs for the pleasure of their brother Snakes. Now they put the Snakes into a large leather sack, which they take to the dancing place, and just before the sun goes from sight, the Snake brotherhood go from the kiva to the dancing ground.

"Salish, that is a great dance. I wish you could see it. The Snake brotherhood take the Snakes from the sack, the Snakes That Rattle, and dance about with them held by the back between their teeth!"

A murmur like the wind in the pines ran through the assembly. To take snakes in the teeth was beyond comprehension!

"When the last dance song is ended, they quickly carry all the Snakes back to the places from which they were taken.

"And this, Salish, is the story of the dance of the Snakes and the songs to them, which bring rain for the corn."

As the speaker sat down, every one began to talk at once. They could not understand the

SONG TO THE SNAKES

Hai - i - yĕ, hai - i - yĕ,...... hai - i - yĕ;

Hai - i - wĕ, hai - i - wĕ,......... hai - i - wĕ.

Hosh-kĕ, hosh-kĕ, pi - na - wi ma-sow - a...... to - mi!

Hurry, hurry, brother snakes, to the underworld, and send us rain.

song which made of the snake a brother. That must be truly wonderful medicine! Certainly the traveler had seen much and should be a good friend to have in their camp. Lone Pine stood up, and in a loud voice quieted the people:

"Salish, this is a story of powerful medicine. We cannot understand it, but certainly the knowledge and the songs of our friend should bring us much good fortune and many buffalo. Now we will make glad our hearts in the dance."

At once the singers began to beat the drum with great enthusiasm, and the night was one of joy and excitement.

THE SNAKE BROTHERS

Kukúsim was very sleepy in the morning, and wished he did not have to get up and go to the river to bathe with his father. The many nights of dancing had made heavy his eyes and tired his feet. While he was yet half asleep, he heard the herald calling out:

"Women, get ready to move! Tomorrow we start on the journey to the buffalo country. Young men, find the horses, bring them close, that tomorrow we may get them quickly!"

Kukúsim had to be told a second time that it was not good to hold on to the sleep, and to be up and off to the river. Quickly he jumped up and ran toward the river, but his father and the two guests were already in the water, and they laughed at him.

"Kukúsim is not a man," chaffed Four Moons. "He sleeps like a baby. He cannot dance in the night and then be ready for the swim. He will have to get a strong heart before he can be a warrior."

He determined that, another day, he would be awake and ahead of the men, that they might find no chance for ridicule.

Now that the cold water had thoroughly awakened him, he thought of the stories of the snakes, and the many questions he wanted to ask. At breakfast there was much talk of the plans for the hunting expedition, but soon he found an opportunity, and asked, "Can we go again for the last time to the snares?"

His mother heard the question and chided him: "Son, you will make your Grandfather angry with your continual questions. He cannot give all his thoughts to a child like you."

But the Clayoquot smiled and said they could go for a short time, and then he would have to look after his horses and prepare for the journey.

Dancing with the snakes

A Hopi matron

"Grandfather," cried Kukúsim, eagerly, "I have ridden my father's fastest race-horse. May I help you get your horses?"

"My Grandson, we will go first to the snares, and then we will find the horses."

They went to one snare after the other. In one they found a rabbit; the others were undisturbed.

"We will spring them," said the boy, thoughtfully, "and while we are away the rabbits can play as they like, with no danger from the traps."

When the last snare was passed the old man said, "Now, Grandson, we will sit again by the big pine."

They were scarcely seated, when Kukúsim asked, "Grandfather, does I-tsík-ba-dish know of the snakes?"

"Yes, my Grandson. If the Apsaroke are right, there is nothing which he does not know. As I told you, he is the one who made all things, does all things, sees all things, hears all things. But the Hopi, the people of the Snakes, do not

Hopi sunrise

know of I-tsík-ba-dish. They sing their songs to many gods, and the greatest is Táwa, as they call the Sun."

"But is he the same as I-tsík-ba-dish, Grandfather? Does he see all things?"

"I think he does, my Grandson."

"Do the Hopi think so?"

"The Hopi do not say it in the same way, but I think they believe he sees all things. Each morning every Hopi prays to the Sun and makes an offering of corn meal. Standing on the edge of the high cliffs on which they live, they gaze toward the east, and as the Sun appears, each one tosses a pinch of corn meal into the air, and prays for health, long life, and good thoughts."

"Did you take the Snakes in your hands?"

"Yes, Grandson."

"And they did not bite you? And if we found a Snake now would you take it up in your hands?"

"No, Grandson. I am away from my Snake brothers. The Snake might not know me, and would bite me, and I should die."

"Were some of the Snake brothers boys like me?"

"Yes, and years younger."

"And they held them in their hands and took them in their teeth! Do the Snake songs always bring the rain?"

"They say so, and the rain nearly always comes. But the white-faced singer laughed at the songs of the Snakes, and said they did not bring the rain."

"Do the Hopi have other songs and dances, Grandfather?"

"So many, my Grandson, that it would take many moons to tell you of them. In some of the dances boys like you, and much smaller, take part, and later I will tell you of these."

"And do they have stories of the long ago, when the animals and men talked together?"

"Many of them; and before we go I will tell you one of their long ago stories."

A Hopi prayer altar

THE GIRL AND THE WITCH PEOPLE

"Long ago, say the Hopi, Yellow Bird, a very pretty maiden, lived in one of those ancient villages. Just across the narrow street lived a family of witches, and one of them was a beautiful girl.

"The witch girl had a lover, and it happened that Yellow Bird fell in love with him and won him. This angered the witch family, and they planned to get rid of Yellow Bird. By witchcraft they took her heart away, and she died after a brief illness.

"Her elder brother believed that she had died by witchcraft, and in the night he went with bow and arrows to watch near the grave. Soon he heard the howling of a wolf. It came nearer and nearer, and then there was the barking of many coyotes. The wolf reached the grave first, and the coyotes came flocking in. These were really witches, who had turned themselves into wolf and coyotes.

"They soon uncovered the body and carried it away. The young man, following, saw them lift a large clump of long grass and disappear into the earth. He looked down in the hole and saw many people sitting in a circle.

"As he wondered what to do, he thought of the war chief, whose duty it was to help in such a case. So he ran up the steep trail to the village and told the news to the war chief. The warrior put on his war cap and his deerskin mantle, took his war club, and went with the young man.

"In the hole through which the witch people had gone they found a ladder, and they went down. The witch people were just ending their smoke. Their chief, a huge, ugly, bald-headed man, said, 'It is time to get at our work.'

A Hopi war chief

"They laid the girl's body out on a blanket and began to sing. First they made her come to life, and then they prepared to change her into an animal.

"But suddenly the young man darted out of the shadow where he had been hiding. He dragged his sister away from the witches and sat down again beside the war chief.

"The witch chief demanded: 'How is it that you have entered our house? Nobody has ever done this before. Perhaps you think you are a strong man. We will see if you are.'

"It was now to be a contest of magic between the two chiefs, and the witch chief was to be the

first to show his power. He ordered that the fire be put out. Quickly then the war chief placed the youth at his left and the girl at his right, and he set up his war shield in front of them all. The witch chief told his people to get their weapons ready. The Hopi witches, so they say, throw small pointed shells, porcupine quills, and cactus thorns. One never feels it when struck by

Hopi flute ceremony

these missiles, but they enter the body and cause death.

"Now the witch people hurled their pointed missiles, but the shield of the war chief stopped them. When the witch chief thought that his enemies must be dead, he lighted the fire. But while he was doing this, the war chief hid his shield. There sat the three, unharmed.

"The witch chief could not understand it. It was now time for the war chief to show his strength, and he ordered the fire to be put out again. Then he opened two jars filled with bees, which began to sting the witch people. Soon they were begging for mercy, and just before the fire was lighted the bees swarmed back into the jars. Again the witches were puzzled.

"Still the witch chief was not satisfied, and he said they would have another trial. This time the witches threw larger shells, but they could do nothing against the shield. Then their chief said:

Flute ceremony

'I think you are really a strong man! You have beaten us twice. Try again what you can do.'

"The fire was put out, and the war chief used his two lightning sticks, the big lightning and the little lightning. The blinding flashes filled the room and cut the witch people to pieces.

"Then said the war chief: 'Let us hurry out of this place! The witch people are clever, and they may come to life and do us harm before we escape.'

"So they hastened up the ladder, the war chief, the young man, and his sister.

"No sooner were they gone than the witch people began to come to life. They reached this way and that for their heads, arms, and legs. But some of them did not place their legs properly, and were lame. Others placed their eyes wrong, and were blind. Many had their eyes burned by the lightning, and their eyes were gray. And so the Hopi say that the lame, the

Grinding corn

blind, and the gray-eyed are the descendants of those witch people of long ago."

"Do the Hopi hunt the buffalo?" asked Kukúsim, after a pause.

"No, they live mostly on corn. Their hunters kill a few deer and antelope, and the boys and men hunt rabbits. The story of the rabbit hunt is a fine one, and some day we will have that."

"I am afraid that before you get time to tell me all the stories you know I shall be an old man," sighed Kukúsim.

"I wish we had some of the Hopi corn to eat now," said the Clayoquot.

"Is it so good, Grandfather? How do they cook it?"

"In more than twenty ways they cook the corn, Grandson, and every way is good. The most common way of all is the *piki* [pē′kē], as they call it. The women grind the corn to a fine powder by rubbing it between two stones, and as

they grind they sing. Here is one of their grinding songs:

" 'Where shall we go when the rain comes?   Where?'
   Sing the Yellow Dragonflies,
   Sing the Blue Dragonflies.
'Clouds are rising in the sky,
   Rain clouds are standing in all directions.
The rain is ready to come.'

   "This they sing in order to make the rain come and furnish them with corn for more meal.

   "They go to the grinding-rooms just at daylight, and the songs tell of the coming of the day, of butterflies, and of the bright sunshine. Every day the girls work at the mealing stones in this way.

   "In making píki the mothers put some of the fine meal into a large earthen bowl and mix it into a thick soup. Then they take it to a baking-room, where they build a fire under a slab of stone. When the stone is hot, they quickly spread upon it a handful of the thick soup, and in a moment it is baked. It is a thin sheet, no thicker than the leaf of a tree.

"Píki is usually made from blue corn, but sometimes they use white corn, coloring it with dried flowers to make the píki yellow or red.

"Also from the ground meal they make many other kinds of bread and puddings. When the corn is half ripe, the men dig a deep hole in the g r o u n d, and in it they keep a hot fire until the walls of the hole are red hot. They t h r o w in the ears of c o r n with the thick green husks on them and cover them up, leaving t h e m t o cook for a long time. That is a f i n e way to cook half-ripe corn.

Baking píki

"But we must not tell more stories today, Grandson. It is time to find the horses."

BREAKING CAMP

EARLY in the day the young men had ridden out in many directions to the meadows, to search for the bands of horses and drive them toward the camp, and by this time the herd was not far away.

"My father," stated Kukúsim, "says that when he was a boy they had no horses, and that when they traveled every one walked, and dogs were used to carry the loads. At first, he says, they thought the horse a supernatural being."

"There were no horses in the time of the long ago stories," replied his grandfather, "and they came long after that period. They did not belong to the animals the red men knew, but were brought by the white-skinned warriors who came with the white singers. Even now my people in the west have never seen a horse. Everywhere I travel I hear many stories of how the red men got their first horses, and what amusing times they had trying to ride them."

"Yes," answered Kukúsim. "Our people tell stories like that, and every one laughs; but my father says that the old days before they had horses were very hard, and they did not live so well. It was not easy to hunt the buffalo, and they could not take many things of the camp with them. The dogs were small and could not carry heavy loads. And in the old days they could not have large lodges, as the covers were too heavy to carry. But when they had many of the big, strong horses, they found they could have large lodges and live better. And my mother says the dogs must like that, because they no longer have to carry such heavy loads."

By this time they had reached the open meadow to which the young men had brought the horses. Each man who had horses was looking

 them over, to see that all belonging to him were there. They did not yet take them into the camp, but left them feeding in the meadows, under the watchful eyes of young men.

When Kukúsim and the aged story-teller came to the camp, the council lodge was already down, and the herald was calling out:

"Tomorrow we start for the country of the

buffalo! Nine days over the mountains we must travel before we come to the great plains where they wander. To-night there will be no dancing. Every one will find sleep early, that he may wake quickly tomorrow."

When darkness was gathering, Lone Pine, with some of his counselors and the two guests, sat in the lodge of the chiefs, and after smoking the council pipe, they talked of

A Pierced Nose

the plans for the journey and the hunt. A party of their friends, the Pierced Noses, had preceded them to the hunting ground. Some thought the Salish had better join them, and be in less danger from the Apsaroke and the Snakes. Others thought if they remained by themselves they might have better hunting. But the chief counseled safety in hunting with the Pierced Noses. The two guests thought there would be small danger from the Apsaroke, as they both knew the chiefs of that tribe and would use their

A Nez Percé girl

voices for friendship.

The plan was that they should go quickly to the plains and hunt until the frosts of autumn, and then with their loads of dried meat return to their h o m e in the v a l l e y f o r e s t, to spend there the days o f w i n t e r. The women had finished gathering and drying roots,[1] and it was well that they start to find the buffalo.

With the coming of light the camp of the Salish was astir. The women quickly prepared breakfast, and as soon as it was over lodges were taken down, and robes and furs rolled into bundles to be tied upon the pack-horses. Men and boys drove the horses into the center of the camp

[1] The Indians, especially those who did not practise agriculture, depended largely upon roots for food. During the spring and early summer the women spent much of their time in the meadows gathering roots. One of the most important was what the Salish call *ithwe* (ĕt′-hwĕ). This blue-flowering bulb, which we call camas, resembles a small onion in appearance, but in flavor it is sweetish. So plentiful was this plant that certain fields, seen from a distance, were easily mistaken for blue lakes. The roots were steamed, crushed, and pressed into cakes or loaves, which took the place of bread.

circle, and each family selected its own. Men picked out the ones they were to ride or lead as extra horses, and the women captured the ones they were to use as pack-horses, on which they and the children would make the journey.

Kukúsim was early awake and alive to everything going on. He helped to get the horses for both his father and mother. While talking with the Clayoquot, he lamented the fact that he was not old enough to ride with the warriors and the hunters, and would have to ride with the women and the babies.

"The last time we went to hunt I had to share my horse with Sister, and see that she did not fall off. This year Father has given me a horse to ride alone, and Sister has her own horse. Sometimes Baby will be with Sister, and sometimes with Mother, and I will help to watch and see that no enemy steals them."

Now they heard the herald calling out: "Soon we shall begin the march. The scouts have already gone ahead to see that no enemy is on the trail. If they see an enemy, quickly they will re-

turn to give warning. Lone Pine, our chief, will lead his people, and at his side will be other chiefs. Behind them will be warriors and hunters. Let women and children follow close. On each side of them will ride warriors, that no enemy may capture our families. And in the rear let there be many warriors, to see that no enemy attacks from behind. So says our chief!"

Thus the people were instructed by the herald, as he rode about the camp telling every one what to do and the position each should take. Five hundred men, women, and children and twice as many horses formed the line of march on this day.

PITCHING CAMP

THE route was over the mountain trails. Often there was not room for two horses abreast, and the line was miles in length. Then, when they came upon an open plain, many would ride in groups, and the line would shorten until it was perhaps not more than half a mile long.

The children who could ride by themselves were often two on a horse, securely tied so that if they fell asleep they would be safe. Babies were carried in their mothers' arms or in a baby-carrier suspended from a saddle.[1]

Much of the time Kukúsim helped his mother with the pack-horses; at other times he would join his youthful compan-  ions. There was then opportunity for horse racing and all manner of larks.

H o u r a f t e r hour they toiled on. As the line advanced, women c o u l d b e heard everywhere urging on the pack-horses. From time to time b u n d l e s w o u l d loosen and slip off. With much scolding and chatter-

An Indian saddle

ing,the owner of the beast would stop, rearrange the load, and then go on again.

[1] The primitive saddle of the Indians had for its horn the prong of a deer's horns and for the rest of the frame roughly shaped pieces of wood. The frame was covered with deerskin. The men seldom used a saddle.

A meadow camp

Near midday they came to a beautiful mountain stream flowing through a meadow of rich grass and flowers. Here they halted for a time, that the horses might rest and feed. Children were taken down to rest, and in a moment the stream was filled with laughing, chattering brown youngsters.

Soon the voice of the herald was heard calling: "Again we must travel. Tonight we must camp upon the Meadows of Many Springs. Travel fast, that the darkness may not come upon us. There in the forest at the edge of the river we shall camp. Let the hunters look for deer and elk, that our women and children may have food. Let the head man of each family reach the meadows early and find the spot for his fire."

The scattered animals were quickly brought into place, and soon the snake-like line was moving on through forest and across meadows. As was the custom, the men reached the camping place ahead of the cavalcade, and, selecting camp sites, started their fires.

It was dusk when Kukúsim with the women came over a low hill, and saw before him a large pine-skirted meadow, and everywhere among the dark trees, the glowing camp-fires. All about in the deep grasses of the plain were the horses feeding upon the rich

pasture. As he came close, he heard the confused voices of many men shouting.

"Wife of Lone Deer, here is your fire!"

"Wife of Crazy Thunder, here is your camp!"

So each man was calling to his wife, and the women soon found the places that had been selected for them.

When Kukúsim found his father's fire, Four Moons and the Clayoquot were there. Quickly they unfastened the ropes which held the tired children upon the horses. Many were sound asleep, and even the lifting from the horses' backs did not waken them. Kukúsim's heart was

filled with joy. This was living! The life and activities of the encampment made his pulse beat fast. Women from camp-fire to camp-fire were calling greetings, laughing, making merry, and asking one another as to the happenings of the day.

Matrons and girls were going to the stream to fill their leather pails with water, and boys were caring for the horses. The animals used by the women and the children, and for packs, were hobbled by tying their fore feet together, and were turned loose; but not so those used by the grown men. Their fast horses were kept near by, tethered with long ropes, and moved frequently that they might feed well on the rich grass. For if they were not well fed, they would lack strength for the buffalo hunt.

And now they were in a land where an enemy might be, so they must have their riding horses close at hand. For this reason, when full darkness came on, each man tied his riding horse to

About the camp-fire

a stake driven at his side, where he slept. Then if the scouts gave warning, it could in a moment be mounted and ready for battle.

Happiness reigns about the camp-fire of Lone Pine. The people have traveled well, and sickness has come to none. The scouts have reported the land free of enemies. The medicine-men have sung their songs, and say that all is well and that the spirits are happy. And more than that, has not the traveler from the western water killed a fine fat deer, which even now is roasting by the fire? A boy who has not traveled a long day through the mountains, and then feasted to his fill upon juicy deer ribs, has not known the full joy of being a boy. Large and fat was the deer, but bare was its every bone when the family of the chief had finished their feasting.

The Clayoquot always longed for fish, the principal food of his youth, and while the women

and children were making camp he had gone to a small stream and taken as many trout as he could carry. These too were roasted over the fire to add to the feast.

Kukúsim was surprised that Grandfather had caught so many fish.

"Truly, Grandfather," he exclaimed, "you must have medicine for fish!"

"Grandson, my medicine for catching trout is simple. I will show you. I went to yonder creek, so narrow that you could run and jump across it. At a narrow, shallow place I laid sticks across like this. Then I got many small willows and laid them like this, so that water could flow through, but the fish could not pass. With large sticks and stones I made just below this a basketlike enclosure. Now I went upstream a distance, and then walked, splashing through the water, toward my trap. The fish, escaping from me, swam into the trap, and I found it filled. There were more than a man could carry. That, my Grandson, is the way many of the people I have seen catch the trout. Some day I will tell you other ways to get many kinds of fish."

"Grandfather, I am going to call you by the name of the white-haired man who knows everything. You are Nápiw."

The evening about the camp-fire passed quickly, and all too soon Mother was saying: "My son, it is time you found your sleep. Already your sister is dreaming."

"May I go with Grandfather when he brings in his horse, before I look for my sleep?"

"Already you think more of your new grandfather than of your mother," she said, half laughing, half in earnest. "Soon my heart will be jealous. If it were not for the man child now at my breast, my heart would be empty."

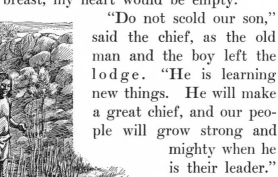

"Do not scold our son," said the chief, as the old man and the boy left the lodge. "He is learning new things. He will make a great chief, and our people will grow strong and mighty when he is their leader."

"Yes, I know. And soon he must go to the mountains to fast."

Hand in hand Kukúsim and his companion walked through the camp and across the meadow.

Fire after fire they passed. Supper was over, and the fires were dying down as the people sought their robes for sleep. Already more than half the camp was resting.

The boy's heart was filled with big thoughts, and he spoke in a low voice: "Listen, Grandfather! Do you hear the coyote? There is another, and another! Grandfather, their cry makes my blood cold, like the North Wind!"

"My Grandson, listen again! Do you hear that coyote call from yonder high peak to the north?"

"Yes, Grandfather."

"Now listen to the call from the peak to the south, and to the east, and to the west. And then you hear their barking from many directions."

"Yes, Grandfather."

"My Grandson, the call you hear from the north, the south, the east, and the west is not the call of the coyote, but of the scouts of the Salish calling to one another. Your father knows what it means, and he knows the scout's call from that of a coyote. The scouts on the high places have looked far to see if other campfires burn, and their signal says that all is safe."

Then they found the tethered horse, and the boy said, "Now we will ride back to our fire."

The man jumped on and reached out his hand for Kukúsim, who with a spring took his place on the horse behind him. In the camp of Lone Pine all were asleep, and as soon as the Clayoquot had tied his horse, they also spread their robes for the night. Above them twinkled the countless stars, and half asleep Kukúsim asked: "Do you think the stars are people? Do you know stories about the stars?"

"It is time to sleep, Grandson," answered the old man. "There are so many stories of the stars that should I start to tell them, the snows of winter would be upon us before I could finish."

"But sometime you will tell them to me?"

"Yes, Grandson."

Then the boy dreamed that he was a star and was looking down upon the camp. His dream changed, and he felt that he, like many stars he had seen, was falling, falling, falling through the sky. With a cry he reached out to grasp something to check his speed. His arms clasped his Grandfather, waking him from dreams of his own.

"What is the matter, my boy?"

"I thought I was a star, and was falling."

"The trouble with you, Grandson, is that you ate too long of the deer and the trout. You should stop eating before your belly is as hard as your forehead."

AN ELK HUNT

To Kukúsim it seemed that he was yet mastering that morsel of his Grandfather's wisdom, when

he was awakened by a gentle shake of his mother's hand.

"My son, you have dreamed long enough. The stars are gone and the sun is coming. Go to the water and make your body fresh for the day."

He felt cross that the sun had come so soon to chase away the stars, but the cool of the water drove away that thought, and he was glad with the voice of the meadow-lark.

Already the herald was riding about the

Go to the water to make the body clean

camp calling out the orders for the day:

"Eat your food quickly, that we may be on the way. There are no lodge-poles to be taken down today, so the women can soon have their horses loaded. Tonight we shall camp on Camas Creek. The way is long, the trail is rough. Let all make haste. Let the young men watch the trail carefully, that there be no surprise by an enemy."

Soon the toiling line was on the way. Today they would reach the highest places in the mountains, and then the trail would be ever winding downward. The pines gave shade to the trail in many places; then it crossed meadows yellow with bloom. The rain had lately passed, and all the world was fresh and green.

Scarface and Kukúsim rode close together.

"These days we do not see you," complained Scarface. "All the time you talk with your new grandfather, the singer of strange songs. Yellow Hawk and Rabbit say hard words when you do not hear. They say your heart has grown too proud, and that a poor chief you will make. Today let us find them and ride together, that all may be happy."

Soon a full half-hundred boys were riding together. In the open meadows they raced their horses, and were roundly scolded by their grandparents. When the trail grew narrow and hung upon the edge of dizzy cliffs, there was no laughter, and they let their ponies pick their own slow, careful way. A misstep here would mean a fall of horse and rider into the canyon, hundreds of feet below.

The setting sun saw the Salish spreading out into the valley of a creek, and hundreds of campfires were glowing in the shadows beneath the pines. Scouts came to Lone Pine and reported large herds of elk, and it was decided to let the women and horses rest for a day, while the men hunted the elk. There were many hungry mouths to be fed. The summer was long, and there was no need of haste.

So the herald announced the plan of the hunt: "Tonight around the fire of the chief we shall sing, that many elk may be killed. Long Elk,

who in his fasting learned the secret of the elk, will sing his songs."

Far into the night the singers sat about the council fire, smoking the pipe and singing, that the elk might not be angry when the hunters took their lives. When Kukúsim went to sleep, the men were still singing.

On the following morning the hunters assembled on the bank of the creek a short distance

above the camp. From this point the valley gradually narrowed, until it became a deep gulley with sheer stone walls.

The party divided, some going by a detour to the head of the valley and concealing themselves behind large trees and rocks. The others scattered in a long line, which extended across the valley and up its slopes to the high ridge on each side.

Then the line of hunters moved slowly forward, with keen eyes peering to right and left, that no elk might break through and escape down the valley. Now and then a hunter would suddenly come close upon a browsing animal, when instantly his swift arrow would go flying to its mark.

But it was the men at the gully who had the best opportunity. Here were stationed the best bowmen—the strongest of arm, the quickest with the arrow. As the drive progressed, the crash of fleeing creatures was heard in the undergrowth below them, and soon antlered heads appeared above the bushes. Then out burst a frightened elk, his great eyes wide with terror, his snorting nostrils distended. As he dashed past the lurking hunters, from either side a flashing arrow buried itself to the feathers in his flanks, and after a few convulsive bounds he plunged forward and lay gasping.

When the game drive ended in the afternoon, more than a hundred elk and deer had been killed. Then came the women to assist in the butchering, bringing pack-horses on which to load the meat and hides.

So great was the success of the hunt that it was necessary to remain in camp a day in order

Drying the meat

to let the meat become partially dry. The women cut it into very thin, broad slices, and such was their skill that the meat was of a uniform wafer-like thinness. It was hung on racks in the sun, and small fires were made beneath. Thus in the course of the day it was half dried out by the smoke and the combined heat of sun and fire, so that on the morrow it could be packed in bundles without spoiling. Then at the next oppor-

The story of the stars

tunity it would be spread out again for more thorough drying.

Great was the feasting, and few gave heed to advice that cautioned against overeating.

During the day, while the women were working with the meat, Kukúsim found Grandfather and begged for a story while they were not traveling.

"Can we not have a story of the stars?" he asked.

"No, not now, Grandson. One should tell the stories of the stars while they are looking. Find Scarface, and then we will take Sister and her friends, and go to some cool place by the brook."

"Are you going to tell a story for girls, Grandfather?"

"Yes. Sister says I should not tell all the stories to the boys, for girls like stories, too."

"But, Grandfather, girls cannot hunt; they cannot be warriors or chiefs."

"Many things they can do, even if they cannot be chiefs. Do you not see the women preparing the meat today? Do they not pack and drive the horses when we travel? Do they not dig the roots on which you live so much of the time? Can they not even fight when the enemy comes?

"My Grandson, there are many stories of girls which Sister would like to hear. Does not your mother tell you and Blue Bird tales through the long nights of winter?"

"Yes, truly, Grandfather, but those are the winter stories, and cannot be told in the summer."

But Kukúsim felt the reproof, and at once found Blue Bird and told her that she was to get her friends, and they would hear stories from the wise grandfather.

When all were comfortably gathered about the old man beside the purling brook, he began:

"My children, as we travel the long trail through life, we find that there are sad as well as happy times. My first story today will tell of sad things."

BAREFOOT ON ICE AND SNOW

"THERE came a winter colder and harder than any other. The snow was deep, as deep as half the height of a man. The old men had counted the moons, and it was time for spring, but the snow did not melt. Ice was coming down the Great River [Columbia] in huge masses, grinding and crashing through the boiling rapids. Every night snow fell and filled up the places that had been swept clean during the day. Snowbirds were everywhere about.

"One day a bird was seen with something red in its bill, and they frightened it so that it dropped the red object. They found that this was a ripe strawberry, and knew that somewhere summer had come. It was plain that something was wrong, and a meeting was called in the house of the chief. After many had told what they thought should be done, the oldest man stood up.

"He said: 'When you who have been talking with words were babies, I was an old man. When I was young, I heard my grandfather say that if a small bird was struck with a stone the snow would never stop. The men of those times were wise.'

"Then he sat down.

"The chief at once ordered all the children to be brought, and he questioned them. A little girl said that she had struck a bird with a stone. She was afraid of the old men in council, and could hardly speak. Then the men talked again. At last they said to the parents of the little girl:

" 'Give us your child, and instead of killing her, as we first thought of doing, we will give her alive to Winter. Then Winter will cease to be angry and will leave us, and Summer will come.'

"Presents were given to the girl's parents in payment for their daughter, but they were very sad, for she was an only child. While she was led away, they wailed as do those who mourn for the dead. The people dressed in their finest garments, and the little girl was dressed the best of all. They marched to the river, and the chief led the girl.

"A great block of ice was pulled to the shore, and on it they spread straw and mats. They carefully set the girl on the mats, and pushed the cake of ice into the swift current. It drifted down, swirling, and lifting and settling with the rise and fall of the water. Above the dull roar

of the rapids rose the shrill crying of the child and the wild wailing of her parents. The people returned to the village, singing.

"Very soon a warm wind was felt, and before many days the snow was gone. Then the people were sure that the words of the old men of long ago were true. They moved away to the fishing places and caught salmon for the next winter, and in the autumn they returned to the village.

"Winter came again. Some old men one day stood on the river bank watching the ice drift by. Far down the stream they saw a black spot on a cake of ice which was whirling round and round in an eddy. A young man was sent to see what this was, and he reported that it seemed to be a human being.

"With long poles the block of ice was drawn to the bank. On it was a young girl, and the people saw that she was the child they had given as an offering to Winter. She was carried to the house of her parents, where she quickly fell

Hopi maidens

asleep beside the fire. And always after that she had the power to walk barefoot on ice and snow."

"So we must not be cruel to the little birds," said Sister, "and strike them needlessly. That is what caused all the trouble."

"But I learn more than that from the story," Kukúsim said. "I learn that when a child goes into danger alone, the spirits will care for it. The spirits took care of the little girl on the cake of ice, and it was they who gave her the power to walk barefoot on ice and snow. Is it not so, Grandfather?"

"It is true," answered the old man, slowly. "And some day Kukúsim will go alone into the lonely places, and there he will get power from some of the spirits."

"But, Grandfather," Blue Bird protested, "that story was sad. Tell us one with a happy ending."

"Here, then, is a tale of a Hopi maiden of long ago," began the aged story-teller.

THE STORY OF CORN-SMUT GIRL

"In one of the Hopi villages was a handsome young man named Rainbow Youth. Every day before sunrise he practised running, and made offerings to the Sun and to the other gods, that he might become strong and swift. During the day and the night he remained in the house.

"One day he announced that he would marry the girl whose corn meal was ground so fine that it would stick to a large shell hanging on his wall. Then all the girls began to grind meal, and to make it just as fine as they could. For all the maidens wished greatly to marry this handsome young man.

"One after another they came to the home of Rainbow Youth and threw their meal against the shell. But always it fell to the floor, and the maidens, one by one, would go away ashamed.

"Now in this village lived Corn-smut Girl, and she was dark-skinned and dirty. Her brothers

163

Corn-Smut girl

teased her, asking why she did not marry Rainbow Youth, and she said she would try. But they laughed and said they did not think Rainbow Youth would keep his promise if her meal should stick to the shell.

"When Corn-smut Girl had her meal ready, she took it in a basket to the young man's house. He spoke kindly, and asked her to enter and sit down.

"Then he said, 'What is it you wish?'

" 'I have come for you,' she answered.

" 'Very well,' said Rainbow Youth.

"He took a handful of her meal and threw it against the large shell, and it stuck fast.

" 'Good!' said he. 'It is my own word. I have agreed to marry the girl whose meal stuck to my shell. Your meal has done so. Therefore I go with you.'

"So the two started to the home of Corn-smut Girl. For when a Hopi man takes a wife, he lives with her family.

"The brothers and the mother of Corn-smut Girl were surprised that the handsome youth had married such an ugly girl, but they were glad to welcome him into the family. When the evening mealtime drew near, Corn-smut Girl went into another room. Soon a beautiful young woman came out and sat down with the others to eat.

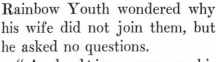

Rainbow Youth wondered why his wife did not join them, but he asked no questions.

"As bedtime came on, his brothers-in-law explained to him that this beautiful young woman was his bride, Corn-smut Girl. Her dark, smutty skin was really only a mask which she wore during the day. Every day she wore this mask, but at night she removed it and showed her true self to her family. For in truth she was not an ordinary person, but a goddess!

"Now the girls who had wished to marry Rainbow Youth were angry and jealous, and they made fun of the young man and his dirty bride. But he did not care, for he knew that his wife was really more beautiful than any of them.

"After several years had passed, Corn-smut Girl said that since she was a goddess, it was not right for her to live among mortal people. So with all her family she one day disappeared into the ground. And at the place where she went into the earth the Hopi now pray to Corn-smut Girl as a goddess, begging her to send them good crops of corn."

"Grandfather, that is a fine story," said Blue

Bird, gratefully. "I shall tell it to my mother, and she too will like it."

"The day has grown old, Grandchildren, and we must return to the camp."

As they rose from the grass, they could hear the herald calling, "Tomorrow we shall travel again toward the plains of the buffalo!"

A BUFFALO HUNT

Six more days the Salish traveled before they came to the prairies where the buffalo grazed. The scouts had gone far ahead, and reported the plains black with them, and long was the talk as to how the hunt should be managed.

If they surrounded the herd with their horses and rode to kill with arrows, many would escape, and little meat would the women have to dry. If they could surround them and drive them over a precipice, they would have meat enough for the winter. Then afterward the young men who wished to show how great was their skill could hunt as many days as they liked with their fast horses.

The chiefs decided that the latter plan was the better.

"Tomorrow," advised Lone Pine, "our scouts will look for the best place to drive the herd. Keep far from the buffalo, that they may not take fright and escape."

Long the scouts traveled on the morrow before they found, at the edge of a valley, a sheer rocky precipice twenty times the height of a man. It stood at the edge of a plain, level as the sea and extending half as far as the eye could look.

When the scouts made their report, the encampment quietly moved into the valley below the rocky cliff. On the plain above they built heaps of stones and brush in two great diverging lines, like a letter V with the point at the cliff. For several days they worked hard at the task, and then all was ready for the great killing of the buffalo.

But before they began the hunt, there were many songs to be sung and prayers to be said; otherwise they could expect no success. So in the evening the chiefs and the medicine-men, after purifying themselves in the sweat-lodge, assembled in the lodge of Lone Pine and sang the Buffalo songs. With great care then Lone Pine gave final instructions to his hunters: each one must obey orders with thought, or there would be failure.

Tomorrow is the day set. Early in the morning the old men, the women, and the boys will go to the plain above the camp, and each will take his place behind one of the piles of stones and brush. Young men disguised with buffalo skins about their bodies and horns on their heads have been directing the herd toward the fatal place, and by now they have the buffalo so near that within a few hours the stupid animals will follow them within the lines.

It is scarcely light when these disguised men are again leading the buffalo. Far and near in many directions are the watchful hunters on their swiftest horses. By the middle of the afternoon they perceive that the buffalo are entering the trap. Then quickly they surround the herd on every side except that toward the precipice.

The animals see the horsemen, and start to run. The old cows take the lead, and look for a way of escape. Men are in every direction but one. Wildly they gallop forward, and the men behind ride madly after them, yelling fiercely; and at the right moment the women and boys behind the piles of stone and brush leap to their feet, shouting and waving blankets.

The stampede is on. Large and small, the animals rush like the flow of a black river between its banks. A few break out at the sides and escape, but the majority run on to their doom. On, on goes the stampeded herd,—cows, bulls, and calves. If one falls, it is ground to a pulp by the feet of the maddened herd.

The leaders reach the brink of the precipice, but if they would, they cannot stop or turn. The weight of those behind forces them on. They pour over the edge like a mighty cascade, and are crushed and broken at the bottom almost as water is whipped into spray. Perhaps a few escape, but nearly all are killed by the fall.

On the next day began the hard work of preparing the meat. Men and women worked together, the men skinning the animals and cutting the joints. The women staked out on the ground the tightly stretched hides, that they might not shrink and curl in drying. Later they would make the skins into robes, lodge covers, blankets for men and women, moccasins, mittens. From the skinned animals the women cut the best portions of the meat, and old women sliced it thin for drying. Even the smaller children worked now, carrying the meat to the camp for drying, and bringing fuel for the fires.

At the end of each day all were tired, and glad when it was time to sleep. For two weeks the meat was dried, and then the men were ready for another hunt.

SCOUTING

THROUGH the busy days Kukúsim had been more than active, and there had been little time to talk with Grandfather. Great was his happiness, then, when he heard the Clayoquot say that he would be one of the scouts to look for the buffalo, and that he would take Kukúsim with him.

Long they rode over the rolling prairie. Then said the old man: "Grandson, we will go to yonder hill. From there we can look far for the buffalo."

"Each time we come to a high hill it is the same," complained the boy, when they reached the hill top and found the country bare of living creatures. "We sight no buffalo, except two or three, which run when they see us. Do you think, Grandfather, that I-tsík-ba-dish warned them, and that they traveled far away from danger?"

"I do not know, Grandson. It may be so. More likely the buffalo that escaped from our

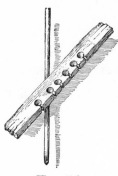

Fire sticks

drive at the precipice had fear in their hearts and led the others away. But soon it will be dark. Far yonder is a stream, and in the shelter of its trees and thick brush we will camp for the night. The brush is so thick that if an enemy passes he will not see our fire."

The sun was sinking when they reached the shelter of the cottonwood trees bordering the creek, and soon the horses were tethered in the open, that they might eat their fill before night came.

"Here is thick brush," said the old man. "Truly no one could find us in this place. In this small open space among the trees we can have our sleep tonight. Let us gather a lot of this dry rubbish to put beneath us, that the sweat of the earth may not get into my old bones."

Their bed prepared, he ordered the boy to gather some of the dry fiber found inside the bark of decaying cottonwoods. Then he took a dead dry stick half as large as his wrist, which he flattened on both sides until it would lie firmly on the ground. In it he cut a slight notch extending to one edge. Next he found a straight

Making fire

shaft of dead willow, the length of his forearm. One end of it he pointed and set into the notch of the larger piece.

Finally, between the palms of his hands, he twirled the willow spindle rapidly, and always with downward pressure. Almost instantly there was a thin line of smoke, and friction-charred dust flowed down the notch from the point of the stick and fell upon a bit of the dry fiber. As if by magic there was a glowing spark, and with a little of the dry fiber for tinder he quickly had a flame, all in less than fifty pulse beats.

While their dried meat was toasting on sharpened sticks pushed into the ground, Kukúsim picked up the two dead and withered fire sticks and looked thoughtfully at them, and then at the sparkling fire which now leaped into the air.

"Grandfather, who first learned how to make fire with sticks?" he asked.

"I do not know, Grandson. There are many

tales of how people learned to make fire. In the long ago time people had no fire. The Apsaroke often speak of the ancient people as those who had no fires."

"How did they live without fire?"

"Do not the bears eat their fill of raw roots and pick berries from the bushes? So it must have been with people in the days before they learned to make fire."

"Without fire the winter must have been cold and hard, Grandfather. I am glad I did not live then. But tell me one of your tales about fire."

"Well, here is one I have heard in the land that lies far to the south.

"When the Creator had made the earth, the animals, and the people, he saw that the people must have fire. So he called Coyote, and commanded, 'Go to the Land of the Fireflies and bring back their fire, for the people have no fire with which to cook their food.'

"The Fireflies lived at the bottom of a deep, deep hole, an enormous well in the solid rock. Its sides were smooth and straight, and how to get down Coyote did not know. But he went to the edge of the pit, and there he found Little Tree growing.

" 'Help me down to the Land of the Fireflies,' he begged.

"So Little Tree sent its roots down, down, down, until they extended quite to the bottom. Coyote climbed down, and there he played with

the Firefly boys. As
he romped about, run-
ning back and forth,
he pretended to have
no thought of the
fire; for the Fireflies
guarded their fire most carefully,
and would let no one touch it.

"Now on the tip of his tail
Coyote had tied a tuft of dry
cedar bark. Suddenly he dashed
through the great fire which always burned in the center of the
village. Away he ran before the
Firefly people understood what
had happened. When they knew
that Coyote had stolen their fire,
they gave chase. But Coyote was
very swift, and he reached the wall
of the pit far ahead of them.

"'Little Tree, Little Tree, help
me out!' he called.

"Little Tree drew its roots up,
up, up, while Coyote held on and

The Kalispel

was drawn safely out of the hole. Then he ran quickly among the people, lighting the piles of wood they had prepared. Thus every family was supplied with fire."

"Now, Grandfather," said Kukúsim, "I will tell you what our brothers, the Kalispel,[1] say about the first fire.

"Long ago the only fire was in a world above the sky. The people held a meeting to make plans for stealing this fire, and it was decided that the leader should be the one whose war song was the best. Muskrat sang first, but his song was not good. Others in their turn sang.

"Near by was a small knoll, from which came the sound of whistling. They hurried over to it and found Coyote and his friend Wren, who had a thick bundle of small arrows. The two were invited to the council, and there Coyote sang his war song. It was so good that all the others could not keep from dancing, and so Coyote was made chief of the party of fire stealers.

"Now the question was, how to get into the

[1] The Kalispel (pronounced Kă'-lĭs-pĕl') were a small tribe, closely related to the Salish, and living on what we know as Pend d'Orielle River, or Clark's Fork of the Columbia, in northeastern Washington. About one hundred of them still live there.

Dance of the Fire Stealers

upper world above the sky. Wren said that he would shoot an arrow up, piercing the sky; then he would shoot another into the end of the first arrow, and so on until there was a long line of his arrows from the sky down to the ground.

"When all this had been done, Wren, because he was the lightest, climbed up with a long rope of bark. From the upper world he let down the rope, and all the others began to climb. The last one was Bear, that greedy fellow, who took two baskets of food on his back. But so heavy were they that when he was half-way up the rope broke and Bear tumbled back to the earth. And so fat was he that he was not injured.

"In the upper world it was found that Curlew was the keeper of the fire and of the fish-weir, and Frog and Bullsnake were sent as scouts to learn in which house the fire was kept. They crept up close to the village, and stopped to listen. Frog was in the lead, and Bullsnake, becoming hungry, began to lick Frog's feet, and suddenly swallowed him with a gulp. Then he returned to the others and told them that Frog had been eaten; but he would not say who had eaten him.

"Coyote, the chief, now ordered Beaver to go into the village and steal some of the fire. So Beaver made a plan with Eagle. He went to the river and floated down, pretending to be dead. Curlew, keeping his watch on the bank, saw the Beaver lodge against his fish-weir, and dragged him out for the sake of his soft fur. When he had thrown the Beaver into the corner of his house, Eagle alighted on the roof, acting as if he were wounded and unable to fly away. Then everybody ran out of Curlew's house to capture the great bird for his feathers, and

Beaver seized the fire and ran.

"Just as Beaver reached the river, the people saw him and gave chase. He dived, carrying the spark of fire under one of his claws so that the water could not touch it.

"Now Curlew sent Spider down the river to spread his net in the water and thus catch the thief. But Beaver swam too swiftly, and so he

reached the rope safely and climbed down. The others of his party followed, and thus it was that the people of the earth obtained their first fire. So say the Kalispel."

"It is a good tale, my boy, and you tell it well," said the old man. "But we have talked long, and it is now time to sleep. And first we must bring our horses and tie them close to us, lest some enemy find them."

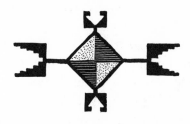

A STRANGE TRAIL

"AWAKE, my Grandson!"

Kukúsim rubbed sleepy eyes, and in a moment was on his feet and eagerly sniffing the savory odor of broiling meat.

"Our horses have fed," said the Clayoquot. "We will eat a mouthful, and start on our day's ride. We will go northward."

Soon they were galloping across the plains, looking in every direction for buffalo. At mid-afternoon, close ahead of them, their keen eyes detected a streak of foot-worn grass.

"Is it the tracks of buffalo, or of buffalo hunters?" the old man wondered. "We will go closer and see."

After examining the ground, he announced, "It is a large party of hunters traveling east-ward."

"Who do you think they are, and how long ago did they pass?"

"They passed but a few days ago. See how

fresh are the tracks. Who they are we cannot
tell, but we will follow for a time, and perhaps
may learn. It may be your mother's people, the
Pierced Noses. You know that word came to
our camp before we started, saying that they had
gone to the buffalo country to hunt. Perhaps
on the trail we shall find some object which will
tell us who they are."

Mile after mile they followed the trail without finding any sign by which they could tell
about the party. Then said the grandfather:

"The sun is sinking. We must not travel
longer on this trail. It may be an enemy, and
we might be seen by their scouts. Here on our
right is a very high hill, with some brush close
to the top. We will stay there tonight, and if
a camp is within the reach of our eyes we shall
see the fires in the darkness. The bushes will
conceal the horses and ourselves."

Watchfully and carefully they made their way
to the summit. Crouching there in the protection
of the dark, scrubby trees, they studied the country in every direction.

"My eyes find nothing in the distance, Grandson, but I see that the scouts of the unknown
have been here before us to spy out the land.
See where their horses' feet have broken the
ground. We will sleep here tonight."

"And shall we make a fire?"

"Not tonight. An enemy might see it. We
are like scouts, and must have no light. When

it is dark and the stars come out, we must look long with strong eyes to find the camp-fires of the unknown."

"You say when the stars come out. Do you remember that you promised to tell me a story of the stars some night when we could see them? Tonight the sky is clear."

So, as they munched their dry, uncooked meat, the old man related the Star Story of the Puyallup.[1]

"There were two sisters who, working together, kept their household supplied with fern roots. At times they camped out overnight, being too far from home to return.

"One night, after they had arranged their beds, they lay gazing up at the stars. They wondered who the stars were and how they lived.

"Tapát, the younger, said: 'Do you see that

[1] The Puyallup (pronounced Pu-yăl'-lŭp) are a Puget Sound tribe formerly occupying the valley of Puyallup River and the adjacent shores of the sound, including the site of the city of Tacoma.

little red star? You may have him for your husband, but that big bright one is the one I want for mine. I wish we were married to them, truly!'

" 'Oh, be quiet!' scolded Yásidbish. 'Why do you talk that way?'

"Soon they fell asleep. In the morning they awakened early, and found themselves in the land of the Star people. Beside each lay a husband, the very one they had talked about in the night. But the red Star, husband of the elder sister, was a handsome young man, while the big bright Star was old and white-haired.

"They were much frightened, but there was nothing to do but make the best of it. As on the earth, they spent their days digging fern roots.

"Their husbands advised them not to dig the longest roots, which, they said, were not so good as the others. But the girls knew this was not true of the earth roots, and wondered why their husbands told them this.

"One day they dug out the very longest root they could find. Suddenly their digging sticks broke through the ground, and peering down through the hole, they beheld the earth spread out below them.

"They decided to escape, and gathering many slender branches of cedar, they twisted a long rope and let it down through the hole. Then, making the end fast, they quickly slid down to the earth.

"Very soon after their escape the elder sister had a child, a boy, who was named Dabábĕt. Every day when she went to dig roots she left the baby in the care of Toad Woman, its grandmother, who tied a board to the rope dangling from the sky. This was a swing for the baby.

"But Toad Woman was blind, and one day two women from the north came and stole the baby. Far and wide the people searched, but they could not find the child Dabábĕt.

"Many years passed. Blue Jay, traveling far in the north, discovered a land beyond this one. To reach it one had to pass beneath a shelf of land which constantly rose and fell like a huge jaw, shaking the earth each time it came down.

"Blue Jay was afraid to try the passage, but at last he mustered all his courage and made a dash, feet foremost. He got through, but not without injury. His head was caught and flattened at the sides, as are the heads of all Blue Jays to this day.

"In the northern land, Blue Jay found a single house, in which sat a man chipping arrow-heads from flint. When he appeared at the door, the man hurled a handful of flint chips at him, almost blinding him, and began to scold him for making a noise and spoiling the work.

"Now wise Blue Jay had recognized the man as Dabábĕt, and he cried out: 'Why do you treat me so? I came to tell you that your mother has been searching the earth for you many years.'

"Then the man rose and with a touch healed Blue Jay's eyes. He told Blue Jay to go back and inform the people that Dabábĕt had spent the years in making many things for them, and soon would come to teach them what to eat and how to work. For the people were very poor, and knew nothing. They lived like the beasts.

"Not long after this Dabábĕt appeared among them with baskets, awls, bows and arrows, quivers, war clubs, fire drills, moccasins, skin garments, and many other tools and implements. He had also numerous roots and berries, and the seeds of countless trees and shrubs, which he afterward planted. For up to this time the earth had been barren.

"When he came, the Stones were people, but he made them stationary. In the water he placed fish, and on land beasts. On each river he put canoes. The huge flies and other insects, the terrors of the earth, he made small and comparatively harmless.

"Many evils he corrected, changing terrible creatures into harmless animals or lifeless things. In the country of the Puyallup, they say, Dabábĕt performed the same work which Coyote did on the Great River.

"After all his labors were ended, Dabábĕt went to the home of his grandmother, Toad Woman, from whom he had been stolen. There he saw a mountain of rock, formed from the coils of the fallen rope by which his mother had

The night sun

escaped from the sky.   And in that land the people pointed out this mountain to me.

"In those days the earth was dim.   There was no sun for the day nor for the night.   Dabábĕt therefore went into the sky and traveled across it in the form of the sun.   But he made the days so hot that the people could not endure it.

"Then he came down and changed a man into the shape of the sun, and sent him into the sky. He said that he himself would become the night sun.[1]

"He announced that he would marry whatever girl could lift his great bundle of tools and seeds. Only the daughter of Frog Woman could lift it, and she accompanied him into the sky.   And to this day Dabábĕt and Frog, with the great bag on her back, may be seen in the night sun."

[1] Most Indian tribes speak of the moon as the "night sun."

THE WOLVES AND THE DEER

THE boy gave a pleased sigh as he turned his eyes toward the moon, which had just appeared, big and red, above the horizon.

"So that is what those dim shadows are which we see in the night sun!" he exclaimed. "Dabábĕt was a great man, and I shall always think of his great deeds when the night sun shines.

"Grandfather, how is it that you have never told a tale of your own people?"

"Well, Grandson, since you ask, here is a story I used to hear my old grandfather repeat in the great house of my father. Have you ever heard hunters say that wolves, when they kill a deer, always leave the stomach uneaten? Yes, so it is, and this is the reason, if we may believe the story.

"It was in those ancient days when all animals were people. Deer and his small son were in their canoe, fishing. The boy fell asleep.

"In a short time a canoe paddled by some of the Wolf people passed him, and Deer called, 'Oh, are you going home?' And in a lower tone he added insultingly, 'You Eaters of Raw Food!'

"The Wolves responded with civil words and went on.

"Soon came another canoe of the Wolves, and again Deer called, 'Oh, are you going home, you Eaters of Raw Food?'

"But this time he carelessly spoke his insult a little too loud, and the Wolves understood.

"'What is that you are saying?' demanded one.

"'Oh, I asked if you are going home,' replied Deer, 'and said that you are having a fine day for moving.'

"'No, that is not what you said,' the Wolf declared.

"They paddled up alongside and dragged Deer out into their canoe, leaving the boy asleep in the anchored canoe. They took Deer to their village and made him a slave to the chief of the Wolves.

"One day the wife of the chief ordered him to sharpen for her two clam-shell knives. So he went to the beach and began his task. And as he rubbed the shells over a stone, he sang:

"'Knife, knife, knife, knife!
    I am sharpening the knife for the Wolf chief.
  Kwsh, kwsh, kwsh, kwsh!'

"As he worked, he thought of a plan of escape, and when both the knives were well sharpened, he hid one under a corner of the house. The other he carried to the Wolf Woman, saying, 'I broke one, my mistress.'

In the wolf mask

" 'Where is it?' she asked.

" 'Why,' said Deer, 'it was broken into small bits that could not be put together, and I threw them into the water. So it was, my mistress.'

"That night the Wolf chief could not sleep, and he called to Deer, 'Slave, come and tell me a story to make me sleep.'

"So Deer sat down beside him as he lay on the floor leaning his head against the bed. After a while the chief and all the others fell asleep. Then Deer slipped quietly out, got the knife from its hiding-place under the house, and slashed off the Wolf chief's head.

"In my country, Grandson, the warriors take not the scalp, but the head.

"He ran down to a canoe, set the dripping head on the prow, and paddled away homeward, singing a war song about the head he had taken.

"When the chief's wife awoke and saw her hus-

band sitting on the floor, apparently sleeping, she gave him a nudge and said, 'Come to bed.'

"There was no answer, and she saw a dark, wet spot on the floor. She looked more closely and noticed that the head was missing!

"'*Ai, ai, ai!*' she wailed. 'Something terrible has happened!'

"Then the people leaped out of their beds, and others came rushing from near-by houses. Some one noticed that the slave was gone, and they began to suspect him.

"Now, Wren was a man who had power to see everything, no matter how far away. So he sat down and sang his medicine song, and then in his mind he saw Deer paddling home in a canoe, with the chief's head in the prow. He called upon Crane to bring out his medicine box and create a fog.

"Then Crane opened his box, and immediately the water was covered with a fog so dense that Deer could not see his way, and becoming confused he paddled ashore at the Wolf chief's village, thinking he was at home. The Wolf men had sharpened their teeth and claws, and were waiting on the beach.

"When the Deer man landed and caught sight of the Wolves, he ran and quickly climbed into a tree. As they could not climb, they began to gnaw off the roots. Soon the tree fell, but Deer leaped into another, and again the Wolves began to dig and scratch and gnaw. But as the tree toppled, Deer jumped into another, and so it continued until the Wolves were exhausted.

"Then they held a council, and other men assembled with them to decide upon a way to capture Deer. But no one could think of a good plan, and they waited for Wren, who had not yet come. At length a messenger was sent to him, and then he came.

" 'Such a little man, and we always have to wait for him!' grunted Elk, impatiently.

"Wren sat down beside him and chirped: 'Well, why do you not think, and make up your mind about this matter, you big man? Such a big-nosed thing!'

" 'I will crush you with my arm if you are not more careful,' threatened Elk.

" 'Try it, and I will go into your big nose!'

"So the dispute continued, and suddenly Wren darted into Elk's huge nostril, and the big man was taken with a fit of sneezing. When the great fellow was almost dead, Wren came out,

and Elk was willing to have peace.

"Now Wren told them what should be done about Deer. First he made up a song, all about the arms and legs of Deer falling down from the tree, and he told them to sing it.

"So they took up the song, and danced in a circle about the tree, and when they had passed four times around it and had finished the song the fourth time, down through the branches fell one of Deer's legs, which the Wolves leaped upon and devoured.

"Then they resumed their singing and dancing, and another leg tumbled down.

"'I pray, my masters,' begged Deer, 'do not eat my stomach!'

"On went the dancing and the singing, and one by one fell pieces of Deer's body, and all was eaten by the Wolves except the stomach. This is where the Wolves formed their habit of leaving the stomach of the Deer. So say the Clayoquot."

Heavy darkness had fallen. Kukúsim yawned and began to arrange his robe for sleep.

"What a scout you are!" said the old man, reprovingly. "Have you forgotten that it is our duty to look for enemies as well as for buffalo?"

A Clayoquot

The boy leaped to his feet, alert and eager at the mention of possible enemies, and together they crept to the edge of the undergrowth and searched the horizon with careful eyes. But no light rent the mantle of blackness that overspread the land, and they returned to their blankets.

"Ho! Grandson! It is time to throw away the sleep."

Kukúsim rolled out of his blanket. The eastern sky was gray.

"We must be traveling," admonished the old man. "Our horses had little to eat in the night, and we will take them down to the rich grass of the valley, where they can feed and drink. But before we start, Grandson, come to my side and turn your eyes toward the coming sun. Look long and closely. Do you see a thin cloud almost touching Mother Earth? That cloud is smoke from some camp, perhaps the camp of an enemy. We will ride in that direction."

The day was still young when they mounted their horses. Long they galloped eastward, and at length the Clayoquot drew rein and spoke.

"The sun is overhead, my boy, and yet we do not see the camp. Watch you the horses here, and I will crawl on my belly up yonder hill and look. Before I start I will arrange my hair as do the Apsaroke scouts."

He gathered wisps of long grass and tied them in his hair in such a way that from a distance his head and shoulders looked like a bunch of grass.

"See, Grandson! Now when I come to the hill top to look beyond, I shall seem to be but a tuft of grass. Soon I will return."

Kukúsim watched the old man creep up the

hill, and then all he could see was a small, dark spot against the sky. He could hear his heart beat in the anxiety of the moments of waiting. Was it the camp of an enemy, who might swoop down upon them?

In a short time the scout returned.

"Leave the horses and come with me!"

"What is it, Grandfather?" asked the boy, anxiously.

"Waste not your breath in questions, when soon your eyes will see. Creep close to the ground. Now raise your eyes, but not your body."

In the valley below, and but a few miles away, lay a beautiful camp of skin lodges, many of them white as snow, others browned with the smoke of many fires. In the meadows and on the hills grazed hundreds of ponies.

"Grandfather," whispered Kukúsim, "who are the people of the camp?"

"I think they are your mother's people. If they were Apsaroke their lodges would be larger, and the lodges of the Snakes are smaller and not so fine as these. My heart tells me that they are Pierced Noses. We will not wait long here. Far down this same valley is our own camp. If we ride fast we may arrive by the time full dark-

ness is on us. Tomorrow our horses can rest.
Today let them use their legs. It is time you
were back at your mother's lodge. She will
have an angry heart that I have kept you so
long."

Instinct told the horses that their heads
pointed homeward, and little urging did they
need. It was hour after hour of steady, swinging lope. When the faithful ponies lagged, they
were forced on with whip and word.

Darkness settled before the tired animals
brought them in sight of the encampment. How
large and fine it looked, each lodge lit up with its
fire and glowing in the darkness!

Kukúsim's mother took his horse from him as
though he were a returning warrior.

"I thought the enemy had taken you, my son!
Do you think you are a warrior, that you travel
so far?"

"I have learned many things, Mother, and we
saw a big camp. Grandfather thinks they are
your people."

"How far away is the camp?" she asked
eagerly.

"The sun was little more than half-way on its

journey when we saw them. Since that time we have ridden like the wind."

"Are there many lodges?"

"Half as many as in our camp."

"Eat your food now, my son, and then sleep. The scouts have found the buffalo, and to-morrow the men will hunt."

"May I go with them, Mother?"

"You may stay in the camp with the rest of the children. Your head has grown large with being a chief's son and with much talking with the stranger. It is bad that you have no real grandfather to speak to you with hard words. Scarface's grandfather is always speaking to him with hard words."

"I like better your soft words and Grand-father's stories," said Kukúsim, mischievously.

"Scarface is not so good a boy as you," admitted the mother, "and it is well that his grand-father uses sharp words to him. Sleep now. We have made words enough."

In the meantime He Who Was Dead And

Lives Again had joined the men in council, and many were their questions as to what he had seen.

"I have traveled far toward the west and the northwest," he told them. "During the second sun I came to the trail of many horses. I followed the tracks far, and to the north in this valley I found a camp. My heart tells me that they are the friendly Pierced Noses, but because the boy was with me I did not spy on the edge of the camp."

A Nez Percé babe in cradle

"If it truly is a camp of the Pierced Noses," said Lone Pine, "we need have no fear, and tomorrow we can kill the buffalo our scouts have found. We need more meat and more skins."

The voice of the council was that they should begin the hunt as planned. Scouts who were known to the Pierced Noses would visit the camp, and if they found the hearts of the strangers were friendly, all would camp together, that the young people might enjoy themselves.

VISIT OF THE PIERCED NOSES

WITH the first light the hunters were off for the plain where grazed the buffalo. This time they were to hunt on horses, and kill the game with bow and arrow. Lone Pine carefully reminded the men of the hunting rules; no one could act for himself, but must follow the orders of the chief, and no one could dash forward in advance of the others.

Scouts went out to learn the exact position of the herd. When they returned to the halted party, all gathered close to hear their words. Each man mounted his fastest horse, which had not been ridden on the way from the camp, as it must be fresh for the chase. The riding horses and the pack animals were left in care of youths and boys.

When the hunters came in view of the herd, it was scattered across the whole valley. As it was impossible to surround the entire herd, Lone Pine quickly ordered that a small band near by be encircled.

Swift as the wind the horses bore down upon the animals, cutting off several hundred from the main herd. Now the effort was to surround the

A Buffalo dancer

band completely, blocking every line of escape, so that the frightened buffalo would begin madly charging about in a circle. Then the hunters, by the pressure of their brown, naked legs, guided their well-trained horses close to the side of the racing animals and let fly their arrows. To kill with the arrow they had to be so close that their feet almost touched the shaggy brutes. Some broke from the circle and made their escape, but few were so fortunate.

The slaughter ended, they began the skinning and butchering, and with the help of the women, who soon arrived, meat and hides were packed on the horses for conveying to the camp. Once more there was merry feasting, and the racks were filled with drying meat.

In the night the scouts returned with the welcome news that the camp in the north was that of Rolling Thunder, a Pierced Nose chief. His words were, said the scouts, that his men were just starting out to kill buffalo, and that they would afterward come to visit the Salish.

Dressing skins

So again the Salish went out with horses to kill more buffalo.

"It is well," said Lone Pine, "that we have much fresh meat, so that we may feast our guests."

Some of the skins first taken had been scraped clean of hair, rubbed soft and white, and made into lodge covers. Many were the new lodges, for a skilful woman could prepare twelve skins in a day, and eighteen covered a large lodge. Throughout the camp, women were busily making new clothing for their husbands and themselves, with which to excite the admiration of the Pierced Noses.

As the time drew near for the arrival of the visitors, scouts were stationed on the northern hills to watch for their approach. At last they signaled that the Pierced Noses were in sight, and returning to the chief they reported that a temporary camp had been pitched but a short ride away.

Tomorrow will come our visitors

"We have talked with their scouts," they concluded, "and tomorrow when the sun has made half his journey, they will come."

Then the herald rode about the Salish camp, shouting: "Tomorrow will come our visitors, the proud Pierced Noses. Their chief, Rolling Thunder, is a brave man, and they are a great people. They have many horses, swift horses, and they wear gay garments. Their women work well with their hands, and beautiful are their dresses and the trappings of their horses. Let our chiefs and warriors, our women and children, dress in their best clothing, and show that the Salish are a people no less proud. Let our maids look beautiful, that they hide not their faces in shame before the Pierced Nose girls, and that they make soft the hearts of the young men."

Time after time the herald repeated his message as he rode about the camp.

At dawn the Salish were again urged to prepare for the coming of the visitors. From the earliest hour the camp was bustling, and about the middle of the morning men, women, and children were dressing in gala costume and painting their faces and bodies. As the sun traveled around to the south, the scouts signaled that the visitors were approaching.

Then the Salish warriors mounted their gaily decorated horses and rode out to meet them. A short distance from the camp they drew up in a line, as if to give battle. Now came the Pierced Noses, who likewise formed in line, facing the Salish. Lone Pine rode out from among his men, and Rolling Thunder advanced to meet him. Sitting on his prancing horse, Lone Pine made his speech of welcome, no small part of which told of his own bravery and prowess, with much flattery of the visiting chief and his people.

He was answered in like spirit by the Pierced Nose chief.

Then cried Lone Pine: "It is good that Rolling Thunder and his people come today. Our hearts are happy. Now all will ride, singing, around our camp, and then our brothers will pitch their lodges in the part of the circle we have reserved for them."

So the gay cavalcade of the warriors of both tribes rode slowly around the camp four times, singing their war songs and uttering their shrill war cries. The Pierced Nose women and children kept their pack-horses at a respectful distance until the end of this ceremony, and then drove them up to the place where their lodges were to be pitched.

HOME AGAIN

For Kukúsim these were exciting times. All
day long and far into night there were feasts
and councils in his father's lodge. In them, He
Who Was Dead And Lives Again took a promi-
nent part, and there was little chance for quiet
story telling or rambles together. When the boy
complained, the most he received was a comfort-
ing promise:

"Never mind, Grandson. Soon the visitors
will be gone, and then we will have many tales.
And the long winter is coming."

With the departure of the Pierced Noses came
thoughts of the homeward journey.

"Let us have one more great hunt," counseled
the men, "and then we will start across the mountains to our own land."

Days were spent and many buffalo songs were
sung before a herd was discovered. The hunt
was with horses, like the last, and many buffalo
were killed.

On the second day following, Lone Pine himself rode through the camp as herald.

"Salish, already the North Wind has brought down the cold, and each night he has covered the plain with his white breath. Men, be ready! Women, hurry in preparing for the march! At once we must start for our home. Soon the snow will be too deep in the mountains for our horses."

With the meat half dried they started. Progress now was slow, for the pack animals were heavily laden with bundles of meat and hides. Each night was colder than the last. However warmly the mothers wrapped the children, they

were numb with cold at the end of the long day's journey, and welcome indeed was the glowing campfire which awaited their halt.

When they reached the high mountain passes, the snow was deep, and it was still falling so thickly that Kukúsim could not see the fourth horse ahead of him. Camp had to be made in the deep snow, and bitter was the work of clearing away places for their beds. The next day came the

At the stream in winter

warm West Wind, and the trails were again free of snow.

At last they were in the pine-grown valley of their own river, where the winter camp was to be. Lodges were soon in place. Then, with a warm lining of skin on the inside of the poles and the outside cover pegged close to the ground, they were warm and cozy homes.

For Kukúsim the long winter months passed rapidly. Each night around the camp-fire brought some new and thrilling story about the animals of the mountains and plains, or the monsters of river and ocean.

IN THE SPRINGTIME

THE arrival of spring was full of moment for Kukúsim. Had he not heard countless stories of fasting and of visions in which strange spirits and animals visited the faster? And he knew that soon he must face that experience.

"Come close, my Son," one day said Lone Pine, "where others may not hear our words. Many times I have pointed out to you yonder peak of the Old Man mountain. We call it so because its top is the first to whiten with the snows of winter. I have told you that it was there, as a boy, that I looked for the help of the supernatural beings. You are shooting up like the willows. You are becoming a man. It is time that you look for the voices of the darkness and get something that will make you a strong warrior and a wise chief. As soon as the snows melt, you must go there and fast."

"But, Father, will I not be lost on the trail?"

"Why lost? Have I not many times pointed out the trail to the Old Man mountain?"

"But, Father, my feet have not traveled it."

"It is well worn, my Son, and you need not lose your way. Feet as numberless as the hairs upon my head have marked the path."

"What shall I see when I go to the spirit mountain?"

"Of that we shall not talk now. When it is time that you start, I will tell you more."

"Could Grandfather tell me?"

"Our friend from the Western Water has talked much with the spirits, and seen many strange people and their ways, but he could not tell. You will see. Every eye must see for itself. Every ear must hear for itself, every tongue must speak for itself. Our words have been enough for today."

Many thoughts came to the mind of Kukúsim, and at the first opportunity he questioned his aged friend.

"Grandfather, when the grass is green again, I am to visit the spirit mountain and fast for visions. What will the voices in the vision say to me, Grandfather?"

"Grandson, you are asking me questions which I cannot answer. I might tell you what the voices said to me, but the voices and the words you hear will not be those which I or any other man heard."

"Tell me, Grandfather, what they said to you," begged the boy.

"It is the way of our people not to show our heart to others," the old man explained. "If we show the secrets of our heart, then is our spiritual strength broken. You are young and the thought is big, but it is like this: Within us, perhaps it is our heart, there is something white and pure, like the snowy down-feathers of the eagle. If we drag this pure feather about in the sight of others, or if we do wrong, the feather is soiled and black, and has no strength. It is the law of our inner self that if we take care of this feather, our footsteps lead us well. When you have fasted on the spirit mountain, my words will be clearer to you."

"Then, Grandfather, I will wait and see," answered Kukúsim.

THE western winds, like a warm breath, swept over the mountains, and the snow went in a night.

Birds sang in the trees, and the hills became green with the gladness of a new spring.

Then said Lone Pine: "Today, my Son, you go to the mountain to fast. I will walk with you a way, that your footsteps start well upon the trail."

As they walked, Kukúsim clasped firmly his father's hand. He tried to be brave, but his heart was filled with a strange foreboding. He felt that he was walking into the land of the spirits, and he was almost afraid. He wanted to ask many questions, but no words came to his lips. At length his father halted and began to speak slowly and distinctly.

"All day you will follow this trail, and when

the sun is sinking, you will come to its end on the topmost peak of the mountain. There you will find a low circle of stones. Take your seat on the edge of that circle, facing the dying sun. Watch until it has gone, and watch you in that direction all through the hours of darkness.

"When the stars look down upon you, build a small fire to keep off the wild animals that might come to harm you. With the rising of the new sun, go you to the eastern side of the circle and watch. Let not your thoughts be of mother or of sister, of food or of water, but closely watch the sun as it moves on its way.

"When it has traveled half its journey, go to the south side of the circle and there watch until it sinks to sleep again. Then once more you will sit as you did the first night, and watch through the darkness.

"Perhaps on this night you will fall down as though dead, and you will hear voices, and you will see something which looks like a man but is not one. He will sing you a song, which you will keep in your heart. To get this song, is why you go into the mountains, and spend the nights and days without food.

"If on the second night no voice comes to you, for another day you will sit and watch the moving sun, and on the third night watch again, as on the first. Then certainly the spirit voices will speak to you.

"When the third day dawns, take the homeward trail. Perhaps for lack of food your legs

will be we a k. I will come far on the trail to meet you, and if your strength is gone, my arms will carry you.

"And when you return to your mother, you may have the spirits' secrets, but you must not tell those. She may ask: 'Did you get a song?' And you will answer: 'Yes, Mother, I found a song.' But the words you will not tell to her or to any one. It will be the secret of your own heart, until the day you are a man and it comes from your mouth at the winter singing in the long lodge.

"Now, my Son, from here I turn back. Have a brave heart, and think well of my words to you, that the spirit voices may be heard. For if no voices come, it is bad. Let not your eyes or thoughts turn toward the camp."

Then Lone Pine retraced his steps, while the boy trudged onward. Did tears come to his eyes as he walked on alone through the forest? Perhaps they did. But they were more of emotion than of fear. Yet what child might not well be filled with dread? He was alone in the fastness of the mountains. The voices of the bear, the cougar, and the lynx sounded through the forest, and the howl of the wolf would make dismal the night.   Alone, he was going through the haunts of wild beasts and toward the home of spirit beings with forms more fearful than that of bear or cougar.

THE FAST

W_{HEN} three nights had passed, Lone Pine was early on the trail to the mountain-top. His heart was anxious for his son.

Half-way up the mountain they met. The boy's step was weak, his face thin and pinched, but his eyes told of victory. He tried to run to his father's outstretched arms, and as they closed about him he whispered: "I heard the voices!"

Then all the world was dark, and he lay limp in his father's arms.

"It is well," murmured the chief. "Now my son has spirit power."

Carefully the mother of Kukúsim fed him and nursed him back to strength; but she asked no questions. Well she knew that his thoughts were his own. His strength returned quickly, and scarcely more than a week after his vigil, returning from the morning swim, he said: "Grandfather, let us go to the forest. It is many days since you have told me stories of long ago."

"Shall we take Scarface?"

"No, Grandfather, today we want no ears but our own."

Their seat was beneath a great tree growing close to an overhanging cliff.

"Grandfather," began Kukúsim, "when you were a boy did you go into the mountains to fast?"

"Not as you did, Grandson. There are many ways for boys and young men to fast, and some

215

day I will tell you what I can of these ways. But today my boy wants to talk. I see that his heart wishes to speak."

"Grandfather, there is much about my journey to the mountain-top which you know I cannot tell, but as to other things there is no law that closes my lips."

"It is true, Grandson. Your heart is full, and there are many things of which you can speak freely."

"When my father turned back and left me alone," said the boy, "my heart was very sick, and I wished that I were at home in the camp, where I could hear voices. Far away seemed the mountain-top, and weary grew my legs. But at last I came to the very top. Then I tried to see the camp of our people, but could not. From the village I could plainly see the mountain-top, but from the mountain I could not see our lodges.

"Now I remembered my father's words: to sit and look at the sun as it sank from sight. Not long did I have to wait until it went down behind the trees. Then truly my heart was heavy. I took not my eyes from the place where the sun went from sight, and before I knew it the stars began to look down on me.

"Then, as my father had ordered, I built a fire. Much wood I carried, that my fire might burn through the night, the dark night. Now I sat and looked toward the west, where the sun had disappeared.

The Salish camp

"Grandfather, I thought the night was quiet in the mountains and the woods. But it was not quiet there on the mountain-top. I heard sounds in the grass, strange noises in the air. In the edge of the forest close by me were sounds big and little. I heard footsteps come close, and in the darkness the eyes of an animal shone like coals of fire.

"An owl sat in a tree and kept saying, 'Hoo, hoo!' At first I did not think of an owl. I thought a spirit was speaking to me, and I asked, 'Who are you?' But the only reply was, 'Hoo, hoo!'

"Then heavy, slow footsteps came through the woods, and I thought, 'Do the spirits walk so heavily?'

"I saw two glowing eyes, and my flesh was cold as ice. I threw a stick of wood on the fire, and there was a snort and a loud crashing in the brush, and I knew it was only a bear. All night I watched, and there was so much to think of that I forgot I had had no food and no sleep.

The Thunder Bird

"When the stars faded, I went to the other side and watched for the sun to come. First the sky was gray, like the fur of a rabbit. Then it grew red, like the flames of the burning prairie. The great round ball of fire broke out of the earth and started on its journey across the sky. At first it went very fast, then more slowly. I thought of home, and how all were gathered at breakfast, and I wished I were there.

"Soon the sun went from sight, Grandfather. Black clouds hid its face. The clouds roared, and I knew that the father Thunder Bird was flying. Then came rain, and I was cold. But in a little while the clouds flew away and the sun looked upon me. Again I was glad, for it warmed me.

"And now it was time to sit at the south.

"When again the sun sank in the west, I built my little fire, and while the stars looked down upon me I heard again the sounds of the forest.

But all the time my mind was upon the stories of visions and of songs. Then I fell asleep, and dreamed of many things you had told me, and of places I had seen. I dreamed it was winter, and that I was sleeping in the cold and the snow. My eyes opened, and I saw that my fire had died so low that my body was cold.

"Then I heard sounds, and my blood chilled, for beyond the dying fire were balls of light, the eyes of many animals. My heart stood still, but quickly I threw fuel on the fire, and as the blaze flashed up there was a patter of many feet slinking away. By the sound I knew they were wolves. Soon their howls made the rocks ring. I think they were sorry they had not had me for supper.

"Once more the owl called, 'Hoo, hoo!' and I waited for the spirits to come, but heard them not. Soon the stars grew gray, and the voices of the forest were stilled. Then I knew it was

time to go to the east and watch for the rising sun.

"Day broke, and the warm rays of the sun closed my eyes in sleep. When they opened, the sun had almost made its journey, and I was sorry I had slept so long. Perhaps the spirits had come close and I had not seen them.

The approach of the spirits

" 'Tonight,' I resolved, 'I will not sleep, for surely the spirits will come close.'

"Once more I kindled my fire. While I gathered fuel, my legs had little strength, but I did not feel hungry as I had felt on the first day. With full darkness came the far-away howl of wolves, and thinking they would come again to get me for food, I made my fire big.

"I remembered the words of my father: to keep looking toward the place where the sun went from sight, for it was there I should see something. And all the time I knew I must keep awake. Long I watched a certain star. It danced before me. It seemed to come close. I thought I heard voices. They were far away, and I could not distinguish them except as distant singing. The singing became plainer, and I felt something close beside me.

"I was not sitting up. I had fallen over as though asleep. But it was not sleep, for I could hear singing, as of all the warriors of the Salish, only very far away.

"Then there was a rushing sound in the air, and the trees of the forest swung their arms and groaned. A man stood beside me. No, it was not a man, for he walked like a great bird, an eagle, and flapped his wings. He stood closer, and I could not move. He picked me up, and we soared away through the clouds over the mountain-tops. He alighted upon a crag, and again I heard the singing voices, and the man who had carried me now led me to them. There came great flashes of light. The ground shook with the anger of fighting monsters.

"Then I felt the cold rain beat upon me. The stars were hidden, the fire was dead with the falling water. But I was happy, for I had heard the singing of the spirits.

"Grandfather, that is all I can tell now. That is my story."

"Grandson, it is a good story," replied the old man. "Truly you have talked with the spirits. When you are a man, you will fast again and then you will know what power the singing voices gave you."

Long the two sat silent under the great pine. The sun sank, darkness fell, and in the near distance shone the twinkling fires of the camp.

THE END

The vision

The above is an illustration from a new book by the same author, uniform with *Indian Days of the Long Ago*. It is entitled *In the Land of the Head-Hunters*, and is issued by the same publishers, World Book Company, Yonkers-on-Hudson, New York.

May we introduce other Ten Speed books you will find enjoyable . . .

In the Land of the Head-Hunters
by Edward S. Curtis

This volume is a facsimile edition of the 1915 publication in which Curtis looks at the Indians of northern British Columbia as they lived in the Stone Age, and as they were still living in the late 19th century. Illustrated with 30 photographs by Edward S. Curtis.

5¼ × 8¼, 114 pages, $3.95 paper, $14.95 cloth

California for Travelers and Settlers
by Charles Nordhoff

A guide to California first published in 1873, *California for Travellers and Settlers* preserves the lost and lovely era that occurred after the Gold Rush and before large scale migration to the West.

6 × 9, 255 pages, $3.95 paper, $7.95 cloth

Northern California, Oregon and the Sandwich Islands
by Charles Nordhoff

A year after publication of Nordhoff's California book, his second book of travel was published. Together they comprise a charming and unique portrait of the life and the land over a century ago.

6 × 9, 256 pages, $3.95 paper

The Mountains of California
by John Muir

"Recommended for all those who enjoy the wilds of America." — *Choice.* A facsimile edition of the original 1894 classic by John Muir which conveys with words and pictures some of the wonder and delight the great naturalist discovered on his first trips into the Sierras. This enchanting volume contains 53 engravings and 14 photographs, including some by John Muir himself.

6 × 9, 400 pages, $7.95 paper

You'll find them in your bookstore or library, or you can order directly from us. Please include $.75 additional for each book's shipping and handling.

TEN SPEED PRESS
P.O. Box 7123
Berkeley, California 94707